THRIVING CITY BLOCKS

*An interactive journal for
loving your neighborhood well*

NATE LEDBETTER

ISBN: 978-1-938633-31-7

Published in association with Samizdat Creative, a division of Samizdat Publishing Group, LLC in Golden, Colorado. Learn more at samizdatcreative.com.

Edited by Mike DeVries

Cover and layout by Joseph Fioramonti
WWW.POSTMORTALDESIGN.COM

Unless otherwise identified, Scripture quotations are taken from THE HOLY BIBLE, NEW INTERNATIONAL VERSION®, NIV®. Copyright © 1973, 1978, 1984, 2010 by Biblica, Inc.™ Scripture quotations marked NLT are taken from the Holy Bible, New Living Translation, copyright 1996, 2004. Used by permission of Tyndale House Publishers., Wheaton, Illinois 60189. All rights reserved. Scripture quotations marked MSG are taken from The Message. Copyright © 1993, 1994, 1995, 1996, 2000, 2001, 2002. Used by permission of NavPress Publishing Group. Scripture quotations marked *The Voice* are taken from *The Voice Bible,* Copyright © 2012 Thomas Nelson, Inc., *The Voice*™ translation © 2012 Ecclesia Bible Society.

TABLE OF CONTENTS

I AM A NEIGHBORHOOD

I am a neighborhood. You might know me as a place, which I am, but I am so much more. I am community. I am beautiful. I am made up of children, seniors, families, and singles. I welcome anyone, and I desire God's peace and wholeness for everyone to enjoy.

I am urban and rural, suburban and sub-urban, and at the heart of life everywhere. You can call me a village or refer to me as in town or across town or uptown. Whatever you call me and wherever you find me, you will notice that many of my characteristics are consistent and true.

I am local. I thrive on smallness, like a radius of four blocks, a one-mile stretch, or five hundred homes. I usually have a name and sometimes I need a name because names are significant, lending to the identity and dignity of a people. Since economics drive much of what I can offer, I need healthy entrepreneurship, multi-use spaces, local retail, and sustainable business to recycle the dollar in ways that benefit me and you and the city of which we're a part.

I have a story to tell. My history, whether rich or recent, informs my development, my tension, and my order. I know that my memory and culture tell my as yet unfinished story, inviting my neighbors to live and forgive as God intends. My healthy homes and buildings seek to conserve energy, water and other natural resources. And my architecture, old and new, reveals my creativity and commitment, my honor, and my forward thinking.

I am led by neighbors. My leadership is shared and diverse among civic and law, teacher and librarian, parent and neighbor, student and partner. My leaders live here with me, generating action from the ground up. My energy is as vibrant as my attitude, understanding that the psychology of my collective self-talk can either perpetuate my challenges or overcome long-term hurdles.

I am connected. My decisions and choices impact other neighborhoods, too. Actually, in the midst of my own brokenness, I realize how inter-connected I am to the story, history, and empowerment of neighborhoods unlike me. Sometimes I appear to be self-sufficient, glittering on the outside, even boastful and proud, while deep down I know real loneliness, pain and empty achievement. Only in humility do I realize my need to learn from other neighborhoods. Only in relationship do I let go of my fear and pride, realizing that the least of other neighborhoods is my greatest teacher.

I am dynamic. Wherever you find me, I am changing. In the city, I can be found in small pockets where life can be wonderful and hard for many. I am discovered in vocational neighborhoods, such as high-rise office communities, and in other worlds, too, such as midtown condos and urban coffee shops. And in the suburbs, I am found among the poor and wealthy, in small corners and within overwhelming sprawl.

I often seek ways to re-engage my age-old principles through years of hard work, waiting, anticipating, and always learning from generations before me. The rhythms of my streets sway and move to the beat of life, laughter and selflessness.

When I am healthy, I thrive on listening, love and intentionality—people are attracted to my walk-ability, my wide sidewalks, beautiful parks and playgrounds, well-lit streets, strong schools, mix of homes, creative business and welcoming style. When I am strong, I am never seen as a place to merely drive into and out of, but as a community to join and contribute to. A community of neighbors is my greatest asset.

And whether rural or city, diversity is my future.

When I am vulnerable, other neighborhoods treat me as such. Churches show up with quick solutions and drive-by service when long-term partnership is needed most, dealers run underground economies that put children at risk, and absentee landlords purchase land and houses as "investments" while local neighbors carry the brunt of the vacant houses, overgrown grass and crime. Sometimes I need neighbors to push through my thick barriers, starting a new conversation to fight for my wholeness. And yet I am empowered most when they take time to imagine new possibilities with and beside me, not for me.

When I am persevering, I invite neighbors to open the shades and step outside with hope over fear, life over death, and humility over cynicism. I look out for those around me, and I will oust the cancerous activity of an individual for the sake of my community. I am a choice of the heart, and I am restored and transformed as people are reconciled to God, others and creation.

As a neighborhood, I am meant to hold people close from all walks of life who are raising children together—Jew and Gentile, Asian and African, poor and privileged, Spanish speaking, and well-speaking of others—inviting words and perspectives that build up rather than tear down. At the heart of community, God's design for relationships, I hold close these words from Ephesians chapter four, *"Speak truthfully to your neighbor, for we are all members of one body."*

Ultimately, I am a parish. Everything about me is meant to reflect God's glory—each blade of grass, each person, each home, and business. I love to play outside, host BBQ's, and celebrate life around the table. I am the host of churches and mosques, hills and trees, concrete and sirens.

I insist that pastors, teachers and policemen envision me as their focus. I need my leaders to live near my children because proximity speaks louder than distance. I demand that churches view neighborhood life as community life and neighborhood planting as church planting, connecting neighbors from street to street, breaking bread and sharing resources, while encouraging people to explore old ways of being church through entrepreneurship, shared leadership, and creative action. And I invite business professionals to view themselves as neighbors through their vocation, finding ways to leverage their skills and resources for the good of the community. I invest into others as people co-invest with me.

I hold community in place. I am Place, and now I wait—for neighbors to reach in, move in, and live up to the greatest biblical command of loving God and neighbor. God is here and moving among families who have been here for decades, compelling neighbors and partners to develop me with hope and healing and long-term commitment.

I am alive. I am breathing. I need you and you need me.

I am a neighborhood.

BEFORE WE GET STARTED...

More than half the world now lives in towns and cities, which is the largest wave of urban growth in history. In fact, according to a study done by McKinsey Global Institute, the global urban population is growing by sixty-five million annually. This represents an annual population growth of roughly seven times the size of Chicago. [1] This unprecedented growth of urban centers poses perhaps the single greatest frontier for the church in the twenty-first century. *Thriving City Blocks* is an interactive journal—a call-to-thoughtful-action among followers of Jesus and people of all stripes, to better understand how to love our neighbors well. *Thriving City Blocks* is built off a single, simple premise: *focused, reflective love leads to transformation.*

Seeking God's Kingdom is a life of process. This journal is intended to be a resource for that kind of life. Reflective love can take years to blossom into trust, push back the darkness, heal hearts, and regenerate neighborhoods. Sometimes even beyond our lifetime. Many have gone ahead of us, showing us the way we should go. Urban elders. Wise counselors. Pastors. Practitioners. Neighbors. The work is challenging, and we face real struggles. But the Spirit's voice leads the way as we learn to practice the presence of God. And as the process unfolds celebration is always in order.

My hope is that *Thriving City Blocks* will be a catalyst for hearing God's voice and loving our neighborhoods.

Journals inherently are a companion for the rhythm of life—jotting notes and questions, thoughts and prayers. *How do we know if we are*

---

[1] McKinsley Global Institute, "Urban world: Mapping the economic power of cities," March 2011.

fulfilling our mission? What are we actually attempting to accomplish? What is at stake? As you proceed through this journal, linger, wrestle, and pray before moving too quickly. Perhaps you want to consider using this resource as part of a staff or team meeting, or perhaps as a personal prayer book among neighbors. My hope is that this journal will be a field guide for you—a place to gather your questions, your reflections, or to build a meaningful partnership, or launch a new initiative.

I write as a co-learner—not as someone who has all the right answers, but as one who is eager to share a process of learning that has been helpful to me in hope that it will encourage you, your neighbors, and the global church. Along the way, we will encounter stories and questions—ones that hopefully will drive your thinking deeper, pushing you to consider God's expansive love for all people.

I believe God's presence is everywhere. It has been said, "There are no God-forsaken places in the world, just church-forsaken places." While this world can get a little crazy at times, ultimately there is hope. While pain and poverty increase all around us, and often within us, I believe there are people of hope—people with a fire in their belly—seeking meaningful ways to live.

The structure of this resource begins with a big picture in mind. We will explore the role of neighborhoods in our lives, participating as neighborhood growers and risk takers, while deepening our understanding of the essence of God's character. From there, we will tap into some practical guiding principles, stories, guiding questions, resources, and prayers as a foundation for the 10 characteristics of *Thriving City Blocks*.

The places where we live and work are dynamic and evolving. There is a sway and movement to city blocks and streets. And with this reality in mind, *Thriving City Blocks* is designed to be a flexible resource, one that can change and grow over time. For while we reflect upon the present-future of our cities, the ancient Scriptures remind us, "There is nothing new under the sun."[2]

---

2   Ecclesiastes 1:9.

ANATOMY OF A NEIGHBORHOOD

I think I won the gold medal—I'm just not sure of all the details.

It was a bright August day, and I had just completed the ultimate up-and-under-flip off the laundry pole. A crowd of three cheered in sheer awe of my skills. I knelt down to receive my medal and then I stood tall. I threw back my shoulders. I had just won the gold medal for the first and only Neighborhood Olympics on Palmer Street. I think the only reason I took the gold at age nine, if my memory serves me right, was because I coerced a vote from my friends on the block.

What I remember more clearly is how much I loved training for basketball season in our driveway as onlookers pumped their gas at the Clark station across the street. I loved knowing many of our neighbors up and down our block. I loved those moments of community when we helped each other by shoveling snow, mowing the grass, or going the extra mile to bless someone else. I loved the neighborhood parade in July and the ice sculpture contest in the cold winter months. And I enjoyed the high school kids who came from all over metro Detroit to cruise up and down our suburban streets, showing off the latest low-riding, greatest stereo-thumping systems known to mankind— or so it seemed.

I was born in Southfield, Michigan, just north of Detroit. I grew up in the west suburbs and played ball at the Boys and Girls Club on Livernois Avenue in the heart of Detroit. Steve Fisher, a long-time basketball coach at the University of Michigan would sit in the corner taking notes to recruit players from our Nike sponsored city league. It was in that little box gym in "The D" where I realized that God was capturing my heart for the city in a profound way. I didn't have words to explain the deep movement of God in the core of my chest. I just knew that God's heart for all people was unity, respect, and relationship. Even though the dividing lines between race, culture, and ethnicity in metro Detroit were unwavering and in your face, I came to realize one thing: we are all made in the image of our Creator.

I am sure there were many neighbors who isolated themselves on our block, and there are aspects of life on Palmer that could have been much different. Every neighborhood is meant to be a wholesome place where children grow up and seniors can thrive with their families, and yet I share a deep concern that many of us are disconnected from our neighborhoods. We are often unfamiliar with how our lives overlap and relate to each other like parts of the body.

It's time for us to ask ourselves, *What is the anatomy of a neighborhood? What makes up the body of a community?* Some traits of a neighborhood are like a skeleton, outlining the physical framework of a given community. Streetlights carve a path of direction for walkers at dusk and dawn, facilitating a sense of solidarity as our streets and homes are marked with warmth and togetherness. Light opens the darkness. I can hear the voice of Jane Jacobs calling forth in wisdom, inviting us to a collective responsibility, "But unless eyes are there, and unless in the brains behind those eyes is the almost unconscious reassurance of general street support in upholding civilization, lights can do no good."[3]

Sidewalks can serve as a catalyst for community life, a path directed to the heart. Urban planners and developers love broad sidewalks, especially if they are planning with community in mind. Sidewalks,

3   Jane Jacobs, *The Death and Life of Great American Cities* (50th Anniversary Edition; New York: Modern Library, 2011), 42.

especially wide walkways and short crosswalks, the kind that allow for multiple neighbors to pass each other simultaneously, are simply wonderful. Jacobs reminds us, "Streets and their sidewalks, the main public places of a city, are its most vital organs."[4] The psychology of our neighborhood is enhanced when we choose open windows over barricades, open-slatted over privacy fences, and open shades as a sign that our lives are open to those around us.

The anatomy of a neighborhood includes homes—old historic homes, apartments, and everything in between. Homes are where hospitality is extended, where neighbors open their doors as a living refuge. Homes are where we can be fully ourselves.

In many neighborhoods here and abroad where pockets of poverty run deep, I have seen the resilience of neighbors taking hold of the beauty sprouting up in abandoned lots neglected by slumlords, pristine rose bushes planted by caring neighbors, and grand old trees that stand tall with pride. Even when a community is environmentally excluded and left to carry all of the "not-in-my-backyard" elements such as prisons, tow yards, recycle plants, toxic waste plants, and land fills, a neighborhood can still stand with beauty. The fullness of beauty is best expressed in the trenches, in the places where mainstream society is not looking. God quietly and willingly unveils the most beautiful attributes of our neighborhoods to those who are seeking, suffering, and enduring.

Neighborhoods are often made up of playgrounds and parks, winding paths, schools, churches, mosques and synagogues, businesses and gardens. When designed well, the walkability of a neighborhood will naturally lead toward connecting people, facilitating the opportunity

---

4   Ibid., 29.

for life-on-life interactions in ways that seem effortless—places where people naturally jump, play, eat and run. These gathering places are the delight of a neighborhood.

Neighborhoods are everywhere, though in forms we may not immediately recognize. I spoke at a university church a while back and we began dreaming together about seeing their campus as a transitional neighborhood. Dorms became homes. Campus buildings became blocks. Students became neighbors, eventually transitioning to another neighborhood in just a few short years. Rather than preparing for some distant future, let's learn together how to love our neighbors now, seeing our neighborhoods, in all their myriad forms, with a fuller vision.

At the core, the anatomy of a neighborhood is much more than a skeleton outlining physical traits. Any neighborhood can display beautiful gathering spaces, well-built homes, and freshly manicured lawns. After all, some of our country's most troubled neighborhoods are among the wealthy, where abuse, neglect, broken families, and loneliness plague those wrapped in the chains of materialism and spiritual poverty. Healthy neighborhoods show clear signs of spiritual vitality, economic strength through local investment, vibrancy in our schools, environmental stewardship, solid city services, including access to reliable transportation, and shared leadership among neighbors. Fueling it all is healing grace.

Simply put, we need to re-discover the soul of neighborhoods here and abroad, where we find a full life grounded in what God intends for our lives. Viewing life through a neighborhood lens could alter the way we see and live for years to come. As we understand how our neighborhoods are connected, we find that we need each other just as God intended from the beginning. Jane Jacobs invites us into this fuller understanding, "We must first of all drop any ideal of neighborhoods as self-contained or introverted units."[5]

What would happen if we sought to know every aspect of our neighborhood? What if we explored our neighborhoods like a cherished jewel, viewing the story of our communities from multiple angles? How would this change our understanding of life, of family, and even church? What if we started a vibrant church movement that focused on the roots of her origins—seeing the neighborhood as her parish?

Jesus walked urban streets, reclined and dined in homes, and listened to the stories of those who were hurting. I am hungry to learn from those who have gone before us as he did—to learn how to practically demonstrate a long-term love that honors the dignity and culture of people, to empower the poor through mutual friendships over demeaning handouts, and to share the good news of God's restoration of all things broken.

---

5   Ibid., 114.

A COMMUNITY OF NEIGHBORHOOD GROWERS

Listening to Jesus followers in other parts of the world and spending time with pastors of the underground church has led me to a concern for the wider church in the United States. What we often call "church" may not actually be what Jesus intended. More importantly, what we often label as something outside of the so-called "church" could actually be the church in action. I am learning to see the church as rest for the weary, a movement of relationships, and as a community of neighborhood growers.

Neighborhoods are like a vineyard, flourishing through water, light, and care. Likewise, neighbors are like care givers for the soil of a community. However, the conditions have to be right for the vineyard to flourish. When residents of a neighborhood don't have access to life-giving relationships, spiritual care, jobs, or commerce, and experience years of disinvestment—it can take many more years of re-investment to see a fertile soil emerge.

The church is called to grow neighborhoods from the ground up, sharing the good news in tangible ways. Together, we work to plant the goodness and grace of God all around us. Beauty springs up where we least expect it as the hard soil is cultivated, watered, and given the nutrients needed to grow healthy communities, block by block.

Scripture is filled with this kind of imagery.

The LORD will guide you always;
he will satisfy your needs in a sun-scorched land
and will strengthen your frame.
You will be like a well-watered garden,
and a spring whose waters never fail.
Your people will rebuild the ancient ruins
and will raise up the age-old foundations;
you will be called the Repairer of Broken Walls,
Restorer of Streets with Dwellings.
Isaiah 58:11-12[6]

They will be called oaks of righteousness,
a planting of the LORD
for the display his splendor.
They will rebuild the ancient ruins,
and restore the places long devastated;
they will renew the ruined cities
that have been devastated for generations.
Isaiah 61:3b-4

---

6   "What is affirmed here is that communion with Yahweh is linked to neighborly attentiveness." Walter Brueggemann, Isaiah 40-66 (Louisville, Kentucky: Westminster John Knox Press, 1998), 191.

As a pastor, explorer, bridge builder, and community developer, I believe we are called to take root in specific locations. Land and love are interlinked. As neighborhood growers, we learn to take the time necessary to know our location, our cultures, the local climate, and landscape. To do this well, we learn to dig into the soil and understand our surroundings. Each morning, as we wake to a fresh day we are invited into the movement of God—planting, pruning, plowing, protecting, cultivating, harvesting, and preparing. We each have a role to play as the Scriptures remind us, "So neither the one who plants nor the one who waters is anything, but only God, who makes things grow (1 Corinthians 3:7)."

While setbacks are expected and storms will arise, we trust the goodness of God as we are about the work of the Kingdom, loving every neighbor within the focus of our "parish." We may or may not worship within the same four walls on Sunday, but we walk the same streets day by day as we grow our neighborhood together. Therefore, our first inclination must be cultivating oneness and unity, while sharing the transforming new life of Jesus with others.

ON THE BLOCK

The block is where life happens in the city. Imagine a giant living room with no walls. The park is where people gather and play. The porch is where people relax and share stories. The sidewalk is where lives intersect. Our focus in this journal will be to live and love—block by block—listening to people and joining with neighbors to extend the hope and peace of Jesus Christ. As we attempt to learn with and from our neighbors, we learn to work out our own salvation with fear and trembling.

While the beauty and assets of the people are often untapped or overlooked, we believe the movement of God's Spirit is always up to something new, calling people toward oneness, unity, and friendship. It is in the midst of this process that we recognize the story of God as always one of renovation, restoration, and beauty. In the face of the challenges we will face, we trust God is writing a beautiful story, one that God has been working on long before we ever showed up.

In a broad sense, a thriving city block could be defined as:

A small, defined area
known as a supportive, desirable environment
marked by caring neighbors
who affirm the dignity of all people
through love and respect.

ON A STREET NEAR YOU

My children and their friends love sidewalk chalk. The playful, messy, colorful, and creative process of sidewalk chalk is somehow irresistible, a sheer delight. With sidewalk chalk, there is always room to discover something bold, to draw a new picture, or connect a line to another friend's line. In a similar way, I am learning that the goal of thriving city blocks is about collaborative change. It is change done *with* people, not done *for* people. It is a commitment to transformation one step at a time—to incremental love as a vehicle to heal our streets. It is through this kind of commitment that we reflect the God of all hope and comfort in our neighborhoods.

And it all begins on a street near you.

With an open-eyed awareness, I am learning to see the everyday happenings all around me—on every street and every street corner. I am learning to see with eyes of possibility. How we see our neighborhood determines the kind of action we take within it. I am learning that a focused approach to love is essential for the peace and presence of God to flourish in our communities.

Our seemingly disconnected suburban and urban communities are beginning to converge, creating a new reality that is "sub-urban." This new landscape is calling for our attention. As we dream big and start small, I believe there is a strong need for concentrated action in small pockets of the city in order to achieve greater impact.

Operating within thriving city blocks are the principles of justice, mercy, and humility. Seeing this embodied in a neighborhood takes time—lots of time. It is a process of people working together over the long haul—people willing to build trusting friendships, working through conflict, forgiving each other, and extending grace. It takes intentional partnership between diverse groups, businesses, and churches with a clear understanding of roles. In other words, thriving city blocks rest on the foundation of relationships.

In the corner of my living room is a hand-carved walking stick. Years ago, our neighbors presented the stick to us as a gift, serving as a daily reminder of our connection. On it is drawn a family tree. One branch of the tree says, "The Strains" while the opposite branch reads, "The Ledbetters." We are connected; we are family. This walking stick reminds me that not only are we connected to each other, we are also an expression of something greater—God's Kingdom on earth as it is in heaven. As we get to know one another, as we carry each other's burdens, we demonstrate the "new family" or "new humanity" that Christ came to establish through the cross—which crosses every barrier imaginable.

As we come to understand the "interior" work of God within us, we are transformed and healed by The Divine Neighbor who is the ultimate example of love through the resurrected Christ. As we change, our capacity to love people and places expands, and the wholeness of Christ's presence will show up on city blocks. Kindness, peacemaking, hospitality, solidarity, community and economic development, vocational stewardship, discipleship, entrepreneurship, education, interdependent imagination—these are the signs of Kingdom movement.[7]

Everyone has a role to play in the process of transformation. Every place has a unique storyline.

As we follow Jesus of Nazareth, may we envision a day when we are known for unity in diversity, embodying the good news of God's Kingdom, and working for justice. May we envision a day when all of us love our neighbors as a way of life, learning from those unlike us, together finding creative solutions to poverty. May we look forward to a day when the most vulnerable of our neighborhoods are freed in Christ, economically empowered, living in safety, and honored with dignity. Let us roll up our sleeves in pursuit of a day when people from all walks of life are playing, living and working together in socially, economically, and racially diverse churches, offices, and communities.

---

7   The reality of these signs of the Kingdom grow from the beatitudes as described by Jesus during his Sermon on the Mount. Everyday life requires loving one's enemies, mourning, meekness, purity, a hunger for righteousness, and so much more.

A COMMUNITY OF RISK TAKERS

Our lives are at constant risk for Jesus' sake,
which makes Jesus' life all the more evident in us.
2 Corinthians 4:11 (MSG)

My prayer is not that you take them out of the world
but that you protect them from the evil one.
John 17:15

I wrestle daily with what it means to fully give myself to the way of Jesus, and more, what that looks like for my family. God has called us to learn beside our neighbors, and that seems to require some risk of relationships. I remember the day we packed up to move to West Side Chicago from our South Atlanta neighborhood. The reality of that moment was both joyful and painful as we left neighbors and extended family that were close to our hearts. Our community risked their love on us, and the chance they took influenced the way we hope to love others. When we lived in "the united states of Atlanta," we were a part of a beautiful community of homegrown neighbors who had lived there for decades. The South Atlanta neighborhood was founded in the late 1800s for freed slaves in Georgia, and now we carry that heartbeat of Atlanta with us in Chicago.

We still cherish the moments we had shared with neighbors like Miss Annie, who passed away a few summers ago. She was endeared to us through her willingness to reach out and risk her love on us—like the time she sent over baby gifts when our son was born. In remembrance of Miss Annie, neighbors gathered in a circle during a community prayer walk to honor her life. She loved our children, and we loved her.

I'm convinced that risking love is critical in today's global climate, and that risk is linked to establishing the new diverse family Jesus came to establish. Now is the moment to *really* go for it. It is time to dream new dreams, and step up to the risk.

Jesus came to us, became flesh and blood like us, growing up among us, befriending us, risking with us and for us, joining us in our poverty. Jesus embodies risk. So risk is a good thing when measured in prayerful discernment, and risk triumphs over folly when wisdom guides our action. Risk may mean danger, but danger can be safer than never risking at all, especially when discerned and lived in community.

We serve a boundless God who has always called people to make high-risk decisions under seemingly daunting circumstances. The author of Hebrews wrote, "Abraham . . . obeyed and went, even though he did not know where he was going" (Hebrews 11:8). For thousands of years, followers of YAHWEH remained a remnant of risk takers, and the practice continues today.

Even when rest and Sabbath are a priority, stress can sometimes be a normal part of following Jesus. As I read through the story of the Scriptures, there are countless examples of people whose lives were on the line, facing real trouble and challenges, living out their commitment to follow Jesus. Who told me that God is safe and balanced? Could faith equal risk? No doubt. And it seems that walking humbly with our God is a process of risking love for others. To love my neighbor, I must share my life with vulnerability. And as I learn to enter my neighbor's story, I receive an open exchange of risk and learning, my narrative with theirs. We love out of risk and we risk out of love—for each other.

In today's economy, the cost of love is Kingdom collateral with a high return on investment. Becoming a diverse community of faith is a dangerous yet joy-filled life never to be traded once experienced. Risk isn't unique or heroic, but it does require intentionality. Risk extends a hand, evaluates value and explores the future potential of a community. Risk leads to an unexpected creative process where we develop new friendships and discover new dreams. Risk jumps into the mix, launching a vision planned for and prayed about. Healthy risk cares first about the other, putting the neighborhood interests above its own, in the tradition of Jesus.

In God's Kingdom, risk and vocation work together, searching for places where God-given talents find expression in the love of neighbor. Exploring the frontiers of new relationships, especially across the chasms of class and culture, is an essential priority if the Great Command is to be realized. In this era of history, the neighborhood with its diversity is becoming a central place for life and faith. It is the intersection where the Western church can join our global brothers and sisters as a community of risk takers.

THE DIVINE NEIGHBOR

Praise be to the God and Father of our Lord Jesus Christ,
the Father of compassion and the God of all comfort,
who comforts us in all our troubles, so that we can comfort those in
any trouble with the comfort we ourselves receive from God.
2 Corinthians 1:3-4

Pain does not play favorites. The brokenness of life is everywhere and some days I am left feeling so incredibly tired. Some days I feel pain in my own life, other days I deeply sense the pain of those around me. Sometimes my faith feels weak, and yet my hope is sustained in the One who has been here all along—the Divine Neighbor.

Years ago, I met a man named Steve. He was in his mid-forties and dying of cancer—the doctor had recently told him he had only a few months to live. Steve reached out to me as a pastor, but we quickly became friends. We met nearly every week, sometimes several times a week. One month turned into another month, and then several more months turned into a year. Steve spoke into my life, prayed for forgiveness over pain he caused in his family, and grew in compassion for those closest to him. He did not use churchy language, but he grew to love God with an honest love—one that can only come from the source of all love.

I remember the Tuesday afternoon when Steve asked me to share about Jesus at his poker tournament. (How could I turn down the opportunity to speak at a poker tournament?) The next thing I knew, I was standing in the middle of a packed bar with a microphone in my hand. The energy was electric. The heart of my five-minute message was the essence of relationship. I told the story of the time I played basketball at a tournament in Ivory Coast. The African arena was packed to capacity with over five thousand fans. We knew we were in trouble when we learned that our little hodge-podge unit of former college grads was playing their national all-star team. These guys were good—really good. One player literally jumped over me for a fast break dunk. I have played ball in many big cities and have seen some great players. This guy? All I saw was the bottom of his shoe flying over my head.

Needless to say, we lost.

As soon as the game was over, several thousand people rushed the floor, and a small riot broke out. It felt like our team was about to get trampled by the pushing, shoving, celebrating fans. The police arrived with machine guns and billy clubs and began beating people. It was in that moment that our team grabbed each other's arms and formed a circle. We held each other up against the wave of the crowd around us. It was only then that I knew everything would be okay.

As I finished the story in that bar, everyone locked arms and surrounded our friend, Steve. That evening, at a poker game in an old building off the beaten path, the Divine Neighbor met us in a very tangible way. Hard-working people stood beside a man and his family saying, "No matter what happens, we're with you."

Sometimes loving our neighbor is allowing our neighbor to love us. Not all stories end like this one though. I have had to face futility in the midst of incredible pain more often than I care to remember. Like the first funeral I officiated. It was for a stillborn baby of some friends of ours. They exemplified a spirit of grace and forgiveness rarely discovered among families. Then there was the woman from our church who called to tell me that her husband had just committed suicide. What could I tell her? There are no words. There was the time when my pastor decided to leave everything he knew—including his wife and children. I can still envision the time when gunfire filled the air in front of my living room, or when my friends continually experience racism and somehow find a way to respond with peace and grace.

I could go on and on.

The list of stories never ends. Some days I still feel pain I forgot was there. Crises abound and it takes a concerted energy just to breathe. There are no easy answers. I will never fully understand the extent of the pain some people feel—much less my own. Yet what I do know is this: God knows my pain and the pain of others—more than I could ever begin to fathom. I do know that there is hope and healing and forgiveness, and that I have much to be grateful for as I experience new mercies every morning.

In the midst of pain, however, we need to step back and observe what is happening within us and around us. We need to be still and wait, allowing the quiet whisper of the Spirit to wash over us with love and grace. We need the God of all comfort to heal us and mend us back together. We need the embrace of the Divine Neighbor. In ways we never fully comprehend, God absorbs our pain. God meets us in the most obscure moments—moments when we have nothing left and the well is empty and dry. God never offers us the absence of pain. Jesus offers himself. He extends a hand as a neighbor. He also invites us to stand with each other in the midst of our pain and our poverty, even our joy and celebration.

Joy and pain are more closely related than it appears; in fact, the two live side by side on the same street—even in the same home. Yet in all the extremes of life, God enters our world. In joy and sorrow, we can experience God as the ultimate neighbor—a Divine Neighbor—within us and at our side. I have come to realize that God hurts with me in my deepest moments of pain and discouragement. I have learned to become a neighbor with others as I embrace God as the ultimate Neighbor. When I choose to receive the unending love and grace of God, then I am able to show love to others and receive it from them.

When I embrace God as my Divine Neighbor, I can embrace others as a true neighbor.

The Divine Neighbor is here, calling us into our neighborhoods. He is inviting us to be neighborhood growers—those who dream up new ways to live and share and lead and love. Just across the street, the Divine Neighbor awaits us with open arms.

Remember to look both ways before crossing the street.

Here we go . . . all together now.

10 CHARACTERISTICS OF THRIVING CITY BLOCKS

Go to the People,
Live among them,
Love them,
Learn from them,
Start from where they are,
Work with them,
Build on what they have.

But with the best leaders,
When the task is accomplished,
The work completed,
The people all remark:
We have done it ourselves.

Lao Tzu

CONNECTING THE DOTS

This philosophy undergirds our life, love, and action as we seek to be a neighbor and bring about transformation in our neighborhoods. As we truly enter our neighborhoods as life-long learners, a few questions remain: *How do we know if we are fulfilling our calling? Are there a few street signs we can look for to be sure we are heading in the right direction?*

The following characteristics of *Thriving City Blocks* are not meant to be all-inclusive, but are offered as a guiding framework for our work together in our neighborhoods. They represent ten aspects of neighborhoods that are thriving, growing in beauty and justice, looking more and more like the Kingdom Jesus talked about. These characteristics are not intended to be a program, a checklist, or a linear process. They are not offered as comprehensive defining characteristics—I'm sure you could add more. These characteristics come out of years of listening, learning, and observing among leaders and communities between cities, cultures, and countries. They begin to paint a portrait of what thriving city blocks look like.

Like a good risotto, you can chop up the onions, heat up your olive oil, add butter, Arborio rice, fine wine and broth, add some sautéed vegetables, and toss in some shrimp—all these ingredients can make a good risotto, but in the end each dish is unique. There is no exact way to make the perfect risotto. So it is with the following characteristics of *Thriving City Blocks*. There is simply not one way to apply the characteristics, as each neighborhood will require its own unique flair.

TEN CHARACTERISTICS OF THRIVING CITY BLOCKS

Internal Change in Us – Beginning first with my own heart

Connected Neighbors – Being fully present as a people of peace

Shared Story – Learning how history shapes the future

Neighborhood-Focused Faith – Joining God's renewal in the world

Thriving Youth and Families – Creating a web of supportive friendships

Empowered Elders – Closing the gap between the younger and older

Meaningful Work and Opportunity – Justice sometimes wears a suit

Quality Housing – Creating healthy, sustainable living for everyone

Quality of Life – Pursuing integrity in all aspects of life

Creative Purpose – Imagining and working together

Among Jesus followers, much has been written lately about being *missional* or living life with purpose. Becoming missional, however, should not be our goal. Our goal in the ten characteristics is to join the mission of God as we learn to become the *new family* Jesus came to establish. In short, our goal is to become the expression of the "new family" with the people we do life with—extending grace and love to each other. The Scriptures are clear that the poor and vulnerable are at the center of God's mission in the world. Wherever we are, let's call each other toward love with the one life we've been given.

As you move through the journal, each entry is meant to spark conversation related to how we can live meaningfully on our city blocks, streets, or cul-de-sacs. Take time throughout the journal for self-reflection and shared reflection. Discern your own unique place, city, and culture. Think. Pray. Jot notes. Ask questions. Start somewhere. Add your own questions to the journal. Share your insights, experiences, and dreams. Use this journal in community with your neighbors, family, church, or fellow students. I have included some Scripture reading under each section for meditation and prayer. These passages represent the story of God's ongoing pursuit of humanity throughout history. My prayer is that the living words of the Scriptures would be an encouragement to your soul, your community, and your work.

Before we begin to explore what these characteristics could look like in your context, there are a few over arching principles to keep in mind— ones that provide the DNA behind the characteristics themselves.

GUIDING PRINCIPLES[8]

Remember God is already here and moving. God doesn't show up when I show up. God is already here and moving long before I arrived.

Be sure you are called to your neighborhood.

Only go where you are invited.

Prayer is the underpinning to life and love.

Enter the neighborhood asking questions rather than giving answers. Listening drives action. Begin by listening to your city block for at least twelve to twenty-four months.

The story and history of every block is unique. Everything connects.

---

8   To go deeper, take a look at the eight key components of community development put together by the Christian Community Development Association: www.ccda.org/about/philosophy.

Become an intentional neighbor. Be yourself.
Have fun. Go slow and take your time.

Identify people of peace on your block. Neighbors
are the foundation to community development.

Seek to understand the felt needs of your city block and neighborhood,
as well as the gifts and assets of the neighborhood.

Build on the energy that already exists around you.
Focus on moving forward the things that have momentum.

Do not get ahead of the people. Local neighbors must
drive the pace of progress, determining the goals, dreams,
hopes, and concerns of the community.

Strive for dignity and character, as these are essential outcomes.
The quality of relationship determines our outcomes.

Communicate with language that honors the dignity of everyone.

Justice and character are inseparable.
We must cultivate our identity as a people.

Neighborhood transformation takes a long time. Veterans suggest ten to
fifteen years or even beyond our lifetime.

Remain where you are, unless the Spirit of God leads
you to relocate. Invest in others by sending and receiving neighbors
who are called to the work.[9]

Seek the Spirit's leading voice with redemptive imagination.
Track re-occurring patterns.

Redemptive real estate is crucial to the process. Buy the drug house. Buy
out the strip joint that oppresses women. Redeem the abandoned lot.
Create quality affordable housing. Dream with your neighbors.

Avoid re-concentrating pockets of poverty or wealth. Isolated wealth
or poverty will only perpetuate unhealthy generational cycles of divide.
God's heart has always been to "tear down the walls of hostility."

Build partnerships in small teams. Do not build a partnership
around one person. Be sure partnerships have clear expectations marked
by a posture of humility, mutual listening and learning.

Invite people from all walks of life to live side by side,
raise their kids together, and learn from one another.

Rest often without apology. Keep a pulse on your heart.
Emotional health is crucial.

Do what you can where you are. Following Jesus is not a competition.

---

9   Check out a new (essential) book called, "Making Neighborhoods Whole:
A Handbook for Christian Community Development" by Wayne Gordon and
John M. Perkins Read more: http://www.ivpress.com/cgi-ivpress/book.pl/
code=3756#ixzz2fD8wjIjr

Explore. Risk. Fear not. Invest in Kingdom
research and development. Be courageous.

We belong to each other. We are a people in process.

Invest in homegrown leadership. Sometimes leadership means
stepping back from the forefront to follow leaders around us while
inviting others to do the same.

Trust, communication, and philosophy are three core areas that will
make or break a team focused on loving a neighborhood.

Love of God is a holy process of personal and social transformation.

We must cultivate a posture of humility, listening, learning, and
friendship in our neighborhoods.

CHARACTERISTIC #1:
INTERNAL CHANGE IN US
Beginning first with my own heart

Guard your heart above all else,
for it determines the course of your life.
Proverbs 4:23 (NLT)

He wakens me morning by morning,
wakens my ear to listen like one being instructed.
Isaiah 50:4

Very early in the morning, while it was still dark, Jesus got up,
left the house and went off to a solitary place, where he prayed.
Mark 1:35

But Jesus often withdrew to lonely places and prayed.
Luke 5:16

Righteousness and justice are the foundation
of your throne; love and faithfulness go before you.
Psalm 89:14

Are you tired? Worn out? Burned out on religion?
Come to me. Get away with me and you'll recover your life.
I'll show you how to take a real rest. Walk with me and work
with me—watch how I do it. Learn the unforced rhythms of grace.
I won't lay anything heavy or ill-fitting on you. Keep company
with me and you'll learn to live freely and lightly.
Matthew 11:28-30 (MSG)

It's been years, but I can still remember it as if it were yesterday. We were sharing a Christmas dinner with some neighbors. The night was filled with laughter, celebration, and a deepening sense of connection. As dinner was winding down, my neighbor Ed and I slipped into the kitchen to wash dishes, leaving our wives to talk in the living room. I have heard it said that some of the most profound moments come in the midst of the mundane in life.

This was one of those moments.

In the middle of washing dishes, my friend changed the subject from something I honestly don't remember to something I will never forget. He began to challenge me in regards to where and how I was stewarding my energy for God's purposes.

"Nate, when are you going to do this full-time? When are you going to make the shift and give your life to loving cities?"

As I struggled for an answer, I sensed in the deepest part of me a lacking, a hollowness. While I was busy about a lot of things, the real questions were these: Was I really tuned into my calling with Melissa? Was I living the kind of life that God had created me for? How was I expanding the Kingdom with this one life I have been given? I realized that it was time to make a major change. The Spirit spoke into "the interior of my heart" through the wisdom of a neighbor.

That was the night my wife and I decided to begin the journey of a neighborhood-focused faith.

I am convinced that the temperature of a community's health is directly related to the health of our interior life. When you and I are in a position of a learner, a follower of God—one who is seeking to be connected to and a part of the larger stream of God's activity—love, grace, healing, and redemption all begin to take place, not only in our lives, but also in our communities. What begins in us flows to those around us, filling the cracks in our community, bringing wholeness and peace.

THOUGHTS

The following questions, as with the questions in each of the following ten characteristics, are meant to spark thoughtful reflection on our lives, our presence, and the transformation of our city blocks, streets, or cul-de-sacs. They can be explored individually or as a group exercise, fostering thoughtful conversation about the issues raised. As with other parts of the journal, take the time needed to reflect deeply. Some of these questions may take a lifetime to unpack.

As you quietly reflect, imagine Jesus of Nazareth conversing with you. How would you respond to the following questions: "Who do you say that I am? Do you trust me? Do you know what I have done for you?"

Then ask the following:

How am I experiencing the hope of eternal life—a life that begins now and extends into the age to come?

In what ways am I growing in character, integrity, and self-awareness?

Am I attentive to God's voice and presence throughout my day?
How can I be more so?

Am I carving out consistent space to slow down, rest, and cover my
city block in prayer?

Is there a time this week when I could pray, walk,
and listen on my street?

How can I listen to and receive love from others on my block?
Am I silently suffering inside? Are others around
me experiencing pain?

What gives me life and energy?
How might the Spirit of God be calling me to encounter
God in my neighborhood?

As the seasons change, where do I sense God's movement
here and in my life?

How are my heart and wellbeing?

How are the hearts of those around me?
My spouse? Children? Neighbors?

Am I living with integrity in all my relationships and activities?

Am I aware of my own "baggage" as I reach out to others?

Am I aware of my story, my challenges, or privileges?

What hurdles do I need God to help me overcome?

Where do I need to suspend judgment or extend grace?

Do I have people around me that I can open up to and
let my guard down?

Am I growing in emotional health and is joy a dominant
emotion in my life?

Am I aware of what is happening within me and around me?

Where do I need to slow down to reflect or lament aspects of life?

What small act of love can I express today?

In what ways can I be present with people today?

Am I learning to be content with my human limits?

Am I experiencing a rhythm of Sabbath?

What day in my weekly schedule can I block out to enjoy God, rest,
and celebrate life? What parts of my life do I need to shed in
order to become my true self, the kind of life-giving neighbor
God intends?

In what areas of my life can I learn to be content in all things?

How am I experiencing or seeing God at work in my life?

STARTING POINTS

As you begin to explore inward transformation, here are a few websites and books that can serve as starting points for the journey:

www.alpha.org
www.CAC.org
www.lovingblack.blogspot.com
www.urbanmissionblog.com
www.transformingcenter.org
www.commonprayer.net
www.richvillodas.wordpress.com
www.godspace.wordpress.com
www.emotionallyhealthy.org
www.theworkofthepeople.com
www.christenacleveland.com
www.nph.com
www.kirkbjones.com

Bouttier, Michel. *Prayers for My Village: Translated from French by Lamar Williamson*. Nashville: Upper Room, 2005.

Elmer, Duane. *Cross-Cultural Conflict: Building Relationships for Effective Ministry*. Downers Grove, IL: InterVarsity Press, 2005.

Hoang, Bethany H. *Deepening the Soul for Justice*. Downers Grove, IL: InterVarsity Press, 2012.

Ishac, Allan. *New York's 50 Best Places to Find Peace and Quiet*. 6th ed. New York: Universe, 2011.

Muller, Wayne. *Sabbath: Finding Rest, Renewal, and Delight in Our Busy Lives*. New York: Bantam, 1999.

Nouwen, Henry J. M. *In the Name of Jesus: Reflections on Christian Leadership*. New York: Crossroad, 2010.

Palmer, Parker J. *A Hidden Wholeness: The Journey Toward an Undivided Life*. San Francisco: Jossey-Bass, 2009.

Scazzero, Pete. *Daily Office: Remembering God's Presence Throughout the Day*. Chicago: Willow Creek Association, 2009.

Smith, Gordon T. *Courage and Calling: Embracing Your God-Given Potential*. Rev ed. Downers Grove, IL: InterVarsity Press, 2011.

Tutu, Desmond. *An African Prayer Book*. New York: Doubleday, 2006.

Vanier, Jean. *From Brokenness to Community*. Mahwah: Paulist Press, 1992.

REFLECTION

Almighty God, sometimes the thought of being still is frightening. I'm afraid of what I might truly find in the depths of my soul. As I begin to take stock of my interior life…

CHARACTERISTIC #2: CONNECTED NEIGHBORS

Being fully present as a people of peace

"Martha, Martha," the Lord answered, "you are worried and upset about many things, but only one thing is needed. Mary has chosen what is better, and it will not be taken away from her."

Luke 10:41-42

One of them, an expert in the law, tested him with a question: "Teacher, which is the greatest commandment in the Law?" Jesus replied: "'Love the Lord your God with all your heart and with all your soul and with all your mind.' This is the first and greatest commandment. And the second is like it: 'Love your neighbor as yourself.' All the Law and Prophets hang on these two commandments."

Matthew 22:35-40

All they asked was that we should continue to remember the poor, the very thing I had been eager to do all along.

Galatians 2:10

My son was born in a parking lot.

Just hours before my oldest son, Levi Mayfield Ledbetter, was born, my wife and I were sitting on our front porch at home, enjoying a beautiful summer evening. I remember children were playing outside and some guys down the street had just fired up their grill. It was a perfect night in the neighborhood. Melissa casually mentioned to me that she didn't think the baby was coming for at least several more days. However, just thirty minutes later, with the pace of Melissa's labor increasing, my dad-like instincts were telling me to grab the hospital bags we had ready and waiting. This baby was coming. Soon.

"Call Amy," Melissa gasped.

Amy zipped right over. Knowing she had intuitive doula skills, Amy was born for this moment. After we called the doctor, we managed to get Melissa outside and into the backseat of the car. Amy quickly jumped into the front seat and coached Melissa while I drove.

Did I mention this was a borrowed car?

It was the summer of 2009 and our van had broken down, so my buddy and former Heisman trophy winner Danny Wuerffel, was generous enough to lend us his car for a few days. "Just don't allow Melissa's water to break on the leather seats," he mentioned. We laughed and I responded, "*That* will never happen."

So there I am, driving 90-plus miles per hour through downtown Atlanta, like we were in some kind of fast-paced action film. Melissa's contractions were getting closer together, and Amy was coaching ever so well. Once we pulled into the hospital parking lot, I found an open space near the emergency delivery area. I raced inside.

"My wife, she's about to have a baby!"

The nurse calmly and slowly responded, "Take your time, grab a wheel chair—"

I left her there talking and ran back to the car. I opened the back door—and there was my newborn baby boy. Melissa was holding him in her arms. Amy's eyes were wide open, "I just delivered your son."

I stood frozen. What now? My son was just born in a parking lot. Well, I ran back inside as fast as I could, "My wife! She just gave birth!"

Pause. "Sir, calm down. She's *about* to give birth."

Another pause. "No…" I said emphatically, "We've got a baby in the backseat of the car!" She finally believed me, and about fifteen nurses and doctors rushed outside.

As people gathered around, I told a nurse that I was the dad and that I wanted to cut the cord. This was my moment of glory. Two nurses leaned in on each side of the car, while I knelt in-between the two front seats. A nurse handed me the scissors and said, "You do realize this could make a mess in your car."

"It doesn't matter. It's not my car."

Later that night, I called Danny and shared the news. He was floored as we laughed together in disbelief. I had the car detailed the very next day.

Upon arriving home to South Atlanta, neighbors began to show up at our door with gifts. In this moment of celebration, I caught a glimpse of the God-given joy of friendship underneath all the day's drama. On one end of the social spectrum, a former Heisman Trophy winner lent us his car. At the other end of the spectrum, our neighbors— with much less fanfare—were bringing bags full of gifts to mark the moment. Here, at this very moment, the lines between people from many walks of life were blurred as we all welcomed our son together. This was a moment of open exchange, of giving and celebrating among connected friends.

Sometimes I wonder what Jesus *really* meant when he said, "Love God, and love your neighbor as yourself." It seems that "as yourself" is one of the most under-quoted and under-valued phrases of the Great Command. As we love and care for ourselves, we are empowered to extend our love for God among our neighbors. Loving our neighbor is not a duty, but a joy-filled command.

In an ancient Near Eastern context, the first hearers intuitively understood what Jesus said as a *communal command*, "Love God, and love your neighborhood as yourselves." In other words, in a culture where the Scriptures were taught and read and discussed in community, Jesus' listeners undoubtedly envisioned this as a communal command. Our Western interpretation seems limited to an individual focus—"as yourself"—but I wonder if "as ourselves" is more appropriate. We are made for God and for each other, and love for neighbor is not only an outward call, it's an inward expression of care and celebration. Love for neighbor is a community in action, where "as ourselves" is experienced through the giving and receiving of life.

THOUGHTS

In what ways are the people around me searching for belonging?

How are neighbors caring for one another on the block?

Am I engaging with at least one friend on my block?
        If so, what does this look like? How can this expand?

How are people connecting in the neighborhood?

Where do we see an increase of friendship, kindness,
        peace, and hospitality on the block?
Who are the homegrown leaders, planners, and stakeholders?

In what ways is the movement of peace expanding in our neighborhood?
        Where are we seeing signs of this movement?

Are neighbors engaging conflict in healthy ways?

What are the gifts of local residents and what assets already exist here?
How are these being used to strengthen the fabric of
the community?

How are we identifying the gifts and strengths of each other?

What do neighbors love about the community?
What areas would local residents like to see change?

Are surrounding neighborhoods connecting with each
other and working together?

What themes or reoccurring patterns are we noticing
on our block or in our neighborhood?

What collective character traits are we known for in this place?

What things do we need to claim or confess in this place?

Are the vulnerable of our communities affirmed with dignity?
How so? If not, how can this change?

Are people's voices honored and encouraged to participate
within the community?

What do we need to be more honest about?

Is the capacity of this community increasing?

STARTING POINTS

Connection and belonging are intimately tied together. In a real sense, you cannot have one without the other. As you explore ways in which to connect neighbor to neighbor, here are a few places to help jumpstart your action and reflection:

www.NextDoor.com
www.i-Neighbors.org
www.myneighborlink.org
www.austincomingtogether.org
www.languageofshalom.com
www.JMPF.org
www.FIFUL.org
www.thesimpleway.org
www.mikacdc.org
www.circleurban.org
www.centraldetroitchristian.org
www.missionyear.org
www.artofneighboring.com
www.slowmovement.com
www.polisinstitute.org (See especially their Dignity Serves Training)

Barber, Leroy. *New Neighbor: An Invitation to Join Beloved Community.* Available online: http://www.newneighbor.org/.

Canada, Geoffrey. *Fist, Stick, Knife, Gun: A Personal History of Violence.* Rev ed. Boston: Beacon Press, 2010.

Gordon, Wayne L. *Who is My Neighbor?: Lessons Learned From a Man Left for Dead*. Ventura: Regal Books, 2010.

Labberton, Mark. *The Dangerous Act of Loving Your Neighbor: Seeing Others Through the Eyes of Jesus*. Downers Grove, IL: Intervarsity Press, 2010.

Lupton, Robert D. *Theirs Is The Kingdom: Celebrating the Gospel in Urban America*. New York: HarperOne, 2011.

Perkins, John, ed. *Restoring At-Risk Communities: Doing it Together and Doing It Right*. Grand Rapids: Baker Books, 1996.

Thurman, Howard. *Jesus and the Disinherited*. Boston: Beacon Press, 1996.

REFLECTION

Almighty God, as we look around and see our neighbors and neighborhood, we sense you leading me us to love our neighbors in the following ways…

CHARACTERISTIC #3:
SHARED STORY

Learning how history shapes the future

He taught by using stories, many stories.
Mark 4:2 (MSG)

He has made everything beautiful in its time.
He has also set eternity in the human heart; yet no one can
fathom what God has done from beginning to end.
Ecclesiastes 3:11

I will teach you hidden lessons from our past—stories we have heard
and known, stories our ancestors handed down to us. We will not hide
these truths from our children; we will tell the next generation about the
glorious deeds of the Lord, about his power and his mighty wonders.
Psalm 78:2-4 (NLT)

Walking down the block with a few neighbors in Chicago, we were soaking in the life of the neighborhood, the history of local architecture, and other desirable neighborhood traits. Like every city, Chicago is a place with a story, made up of multiple stories that weave in and out of each other. As we walked a little farther, a neighbor stopped us en route asking a clear and pointed question, "What are you about?"

This is a profound question directed to the heart. No matter how young or old, where we live or work, this question cuts out the fluff in a hurry, condensing multiple questions—such as, What are WE about? What's our story? Why are we here? What are we living for? And how does our story connect with his?—into one big question that demands a truthful answer.

In that moment, as we pondered what we "were about", a friend walked toward the man and explained that we were local neighbors committed to loving God and people. It wasn't a long conversation, but it certainly held more depth than a long exchange about the weather.

And it's a question that will remain with me for years. It's a question that I wish more people would ask. It's a question that tends to linger for a while until one has a few choices: I can dismiss the question entirely and go about my day above the surface of reality. Ignoring the question would be like ignoring the deep waters of my heart by remaining in pseudo community.

My other choice is to walk toward the question, which is the same as walking toward the man asking the question, making space to enter each other's stories. The man asking the question cannot be separated from the question itself, similar to the ways loving God and neighbor go together. If we ignore the question, our love for God is only abstract in theory. If we engage the depth of the question with our neighbor, our love for God becomes a little more real.

What is the supreme good? What is the most excellent way? "If I give all I possess to the poor, and give over my body to hardship that I may boast, but do not have love, I gain nothing" (1 Corinthians 13:3).

THOUGHTS

How does the story of God connect with our neighborhood?
　　　　How is it being put on display?

How is my life story connecting with the story of my neighbors?

Do my neighbors share an understanding of the block's history—
　　　　spiritual, cultural, economic, and social—
　　　　within the larger story of the neighborhood?

Is there a sense of neighborhood identity?

What does the "self-talk" of my neighbors reveal about them, other
　　　　people who don't live on my block, or the neighborhood
　　　　as a whole?

Is there a strong "pride of place" here? If so, how is this being put on
　　　　display? If not, what barriers exist?

Do we speak honestly and positively about each other, our block, and our neighborhood?

Are people open to sharing their lives and stories with each other, carrying each other's burdens?

What felt needs are people expressing? What does this tell us about the condition of our neighborhood?

Do people have safe places to process life's challenges? Why or why not?

Do my neighbors have a sense of ownership and leadership of the neighborhood's ongoing story?

What are the communal "blind spots"? Are complimentary partnerships in motion here?

Are we open to the next chapter being written among us?

Are we communicating stories with language that honors everyone as made in God's image?

Am I speaking words of life—words that build up?

Am I willing to submit my full life to the Jesus story? What might this look like in my context?

Am I open to God's retelling of my story? Our story?

In what ways do I long for my story to be edited, redeemed, or retold?

STARTING POINTS

Every neighborhood is unique—with a unique story, unique history, unique challenges, and unique opportunities. Beginning to explore this story means we will need to be listeners first. Here are a few resources to help us along our way:

"The Danger of a Single Story" by Chimamanda Ngozi Adichie (http://www.ted.com/talks/chimamanda_adichie_the_danger_of_a_single_story.html)
"African Men. Hollywood Stereotypes." (www.mamahope.org *and also* http://www.youtube.com/watch?v=qSElmEmEjb4)
"Africa for Norway" – a fictional spoof where South Africans make a crucial point about stereotypes (www.africafornorway.no/why)
www.brenebrown.com

Chester, Tim, ed. *Justice, Mercy, and Humility: Integral Mission and the Poor*. Milton Keynes, UK: Paternoster, 2003.

Freire, Paulo. *The Pedagogy of the Oppressed*. 30th Anniversary Edition. New York: Bloomsbury Academic, 2000.

Jones, Sally-Lloyd. *The Jesus Storybook Bible*. Grand Rapids: Zondervan, 2007.

Livermore, David A. *Cultural Intelligence: Improving Your CQ To Engage Our Multicultural World*. Grand Rapids: Baker Academic, 2009.

Tutu, Archbishop Desmond. *Children of God Storybook Bible*. Grand Rapids: Zondervan, 2010.

Wheeler, Houston. *Organizing in the Other Atlanta: How the McDaniel-Glenn Leadership Organized to Embarrass and Lead Atlanta's Pharaohs to Produce Affordable Housing in the Community.* Southern Ministry Network, 1992.

Wright, Tom. *The Meal Jesus Gave Us: Understanding Holy Communion.* Louisville: Westminster John Knox, 2002.

"The God of Judaism is not a God who likes to be flattered in a more or less passive routine of worship; this God is out working the neighborhood and wants all adherents doing the same."

-Walter Brueggemann
Isaiah 40-66

REFLECTION

Knowing our story and how it intersects with God's larger story is critical for us to see our neighborhoods transformed. Take a few minutes to write out (or share) three stories—your story, the neighborhood's story, and God's story. What did you learn from these stories?

CHARACTERISTIC #4: NEIGHBORHOOD-FOCUSED FAITH
Joining God's renewal in the world

The Word became flesh and blood, and moved into the neighborhood.
John 1:14 (MSG)

How good and pleasant it is when God's people live together in unity!
Psalm 133:1

Go to the lost, confused people right here in the neighborhood.
Tell them that the kingdom is here.
Matthew 10:6-7 (MSG)

This, then is how you should pray: "Our Father in heaven, hallowed be your
name, your kingdom come, your will be done, on earth as it is in heaven."
Matthew 6:9-10

Your people will rebuild the ancient ruins and will raise up the
age-old foundations; you will be called Repairer of Broken Walls,
Restorer of Streets with Dwellings.
Isaiah 58:12

They devoted themselves to the apostles' teaching and to fellowship, to the
breaking of bread and to prayer. Everyone was filled with awe at the many
wonders and signs performed by the apostles. All the believers were together
and had everything in common. They sold property and possessions to give
to anyone who had need. Every day they continued to meet together in the
temple courts. They broke bread in their homes and ate together with glad
and sincere hearts, praising God and enjoying the favor of all the people.
And the Lord added to their number daily those who were being saved.
Acts 2:42-47

Monday, July 15
Moving Day: West Side Chicago
To: An open letter to the wider church
Cc: People of all stripes
Subject: Beloved Community
From: nate@ontheblock.us (Nate Ledbetter)

Dear Beloved Community (Come, Unity),

I received your invitation to join the banquet, and I am writing to
RSVP. I plan to attend and I hope to bring others with me. Glimpses
of your community bring me deep joy, because I know that God
dreamed you up at the beginning of time. Although I am writing
personally, I know I am not alone because humanity was made for
you though, for now, it seems you are miles away as I write from a
distance. History's wide wake precedes us and tomorrow is upon us
as I find myself aching for you.

I lament as I continue the process of repentance in my own heart,
asking God to shape me toward the dream of reconciled friendships
between cultures and classes and across any line that isolates people. I
am grateful to know that your invitation is open to everyone. I grieve
because it seems that we, and I mean "we" as in *me* and the state of our
country and, more specifically, those who follow Jesus here and abroad,
have a long walk ahead in your direction.

And so I join my sisters and brothers as we learn to enter each other's
stories, struggles and pain, holding each other up while the One calls
us to rise each morning with humility. I am eager to learn from my
neighbors as a member of an increasingly diverse community that
seeks the heart of God. I dream of Beloved Community to become the

reality of our cities and neighborhoods, and I can hardly wait for the banquet to begin. This will be a *feast* for the ages. Remember that time when Jesus kept the party going by turning water into wine?

The dimensions of your love influences every aspect of life together. Your family reflects the heart of what the living church is meant to be. And your prophetic voice continues to challenge the elite and lowly, the powerful and prejudiced, the prideful and privileged, indeed all of us, to lay down our lives as slaves to Christ. Thankfully, *God's capacity to forgive is unfiltered grace.*

In the tradition of Eastern Christianity, I pray,
"Lord Jesus Christ, Son of God, have mercy on me, a sinner."

In your family, you invite us toward listening, forgiveness, mutual submission, shared leadership, hospitality, and a willingness to give and receive. And I thank God for friends—those who share a similar heartbeat when I feel lonely or do not fully belong anywhere. I thank God for the comfort of the One who brings peace, stirring up new dreams through shared imagination, reserved in the space where those who are unlike each other come together. I thank God for belonging with those who seek the character and depth of God's love to change all of us.

Around the table, we can taste and see that God is good. Even in small glimpses, when neighbors from all walks begin to move side-by-side, raising children together, sharing meals together, pursuing each other's hearts, my hope expands. Even now, Jesus followers are gathering throughout the world—in huts and shacks, streets and villages, towns and megacities. The mobility and adaptability of Christ-ones around the globe is an amazing picture. I love the church. While struggling, she's still radiant, full of hope, and central to God's kingdom.

And so I pray for the healing of our land, for a return to the new life Jesus offers in the midst of the pain and problems within us. There was a time when the church shared all things in common, when people from all stripes were known for coming together. A time when justice and care for the poor was a priority, and love was a way of life. A time when the eternal life of God was shared out of a demonstration that the cross of Christ defeated death, evil, and the lie that only some people are of value.

As I grieve with my neighbors, I lament the systemic sin and aftermath of our (my) collective history. Even knowing the pain of our current reality, you, Beloved Community are possible. God's vision for you is right here in this place, in this era, where the poor and privileged live and work. Maybe you are closer than I realized. May God awaken me to a "wakeful faith," where my eyes recognize you, grounded with resilient hope in the neighborhood. I pray God brings us through to the other side of redemption, where we can look back and remember that this walk is good. You reflect the collective image of God in such beautiful ways.

A day without tears is coming where all will be well again, when God who sees our pain will put the broken pieces back together. Lord, I am not worthy to receive you, but only say the word and I shall be healed (see Matthew 8:5-11). Until everyone gathers together, I await with anticipation while the table is being set.

Much Love,
Nate

"I look upon all the world as my parish." –John Wesley,
The Journal of John Wesley, May 28, 1739.

THOUGHTS

In what ways are people hearing about and experiencing
the hopeful way of Jesus Christ?

What is the intention of the Gospel?

What is my understanding of Beloved Community?

How are Jesus followers active as intentional
neighbors *with* the community on the block?

In what ways can the living church love people
with dignity in our community?

What is the reputation of the church in our community?
Do neighbors feel welcome?

Is our church primarily asking church-centric questions?

What questions are we asking with the surrounding
neighborhood beyond our four walls?

Are we willing to put the interests of the neighborhood
above our own?

Do the majority of people in our community live within
one mile of where we gather?

What is our role or relationship with the surrounding neighborhood?

Are we careful not to make sweeping generalizations, trying not to
categorize every expression of Kingdom activity "real church"
or "not church" or "parachurch?"

How are we engaging issues of displacement among
the poor around us, including the most unexpected places?

What kind of church is good news for this place?

How is the Gospel put on display in our actions?

Does our leadership team represent the changing demographics
of our neighborhood? Do local neighbors embrace the church
as a people pursuing the common good of all?

What common (re-occurring) patterns of God's movement are
we noticing in our city, within our neighborhood,
or on our block or street?

How are these patterns on display in our city, neighborhood, or block?

Are churches and other faith expressions working together as
neighbors? If so, how? If not, what are some of the reasons?

Are we tuned into each other's heart and struggles?

How is the body of Christ expressing unity and oneness in our
neighborhood and throughout the city?

Is the church focused on long-term partnership, co-investment,
and community development beyond only relief
and mercy services? How so?

Is there an awareness of people's pain individually,
collectively, systemically and historically?

In what ways are people caring for one another
inwardly and outwardly?

How might moments of solitude and silence blend with
a community's redemptive imagination?

Are we demonstrating a physical expression of God's love?

Do we have a theology of suffering? What is it?

Is this conversation limited to our own concentric circles?

Does our theology reflect multi-ethnic and global viewpoints?

Are we open to the new thing God is doing in a new way?

Are we becoming the kind of church God dreams of?

STARTING POINTS

The Kingdom of God is a movement—a movement of people living in the way of Jesus. Love. Grace. Acceptance. Sacrifice. Redemption. These need to be more than words. They need to be visible expressions announcing to all who see them, "The Kingdom of God has come near." The following are places to start in gaining a vision for what it means to join God's renewal in our neighborhoods:

www.lambschurch.org
www.latinoleadershipcircle.typepad.com
www.theforgottenways.org
www.releasetheape.com
www.evangelicalimmigrationtable.com
www.parishcollective.com
www.weare3dm.com
www.ncmi.org
www.exponential.org
www.redletterchristians.org

Adeyemo, Tokunboh, ed. *The African Bible Commentary: A One-Volume Commentary Written by 70 African Scholars*. 2d ed. Grand Rapids: Zondervan, 2010.

Boone, Dan. *The Church in Exile: Interpreting Where We Are*. Oklahoma City: Dust Jacket Press, 2012.

Carroll R., M. Daniel. *Christians at the Border: Immigration, the Church, and the Bible*. Grand Rapids: Baker Academic, 2008.

Chandler, Paul-Gordon. *God's Global Mosaic: What We Can Learn from Christians Around the World*. Downers Grove, IL: Intervarsity Press, 2000.

Hunsberger, George R. and Craig Van Gelder, eds. *The Church Between Gospel and Culture: The Emerging Mission in North America*. Grand Rapids: Eerdmans, 1997.

Jenkins, Philip. *The Next Christendom: The Coming of Global Christianity*. 3d ed. New York: Oxford University Press, 2011.

Kling, Fritz. *The Meeting of the Waters: 7 Global Currents That Will Propel the Future Church*. Colorado Springs: David C. Cook, 2010.

Lyons, Gabe. *The Next Christians: Seven Ways You Can Live the Gospel and Restore the World*. Colorado Springs: Multnomah, 2012.

Marsh, Charles. *The Beloved Community: How Faith Shapes Social Justice from the Civil Rights Movement to Today*. New York: Basic Books, 2005.

Martin, Jim. *The Just Church: Becoming a Risk-Taking, Justice-Seeking, Disciple-Making Congregation*. Carol Stream: Tyndale Momentum, 2012.

Park, Sydney M., Soong-Chan Rah, and Al Tizon, eds. *Honoring the Generations: Learning with Asian North American Congregations*. Valley Forge: Judson Press, 2012.

Rah, Soong-Chan. *The Next Evangelicalism: Freeing the Church from Western Cultural Captivity*. Downers Grove, IL: InterVarsity Press, 2009.

Smith, Efrem and Phil Jackson. *The Hip Hop Church: Connecting with the Movement Shaping Our Culture*. Downers Grove, IL: InterVarsity Press, 2006.

Spencer, Aida Besancon and William David Spencer, eds. *The Global God: Multicultural Evangelical Views of God*. Grand Rapids: Baker Academic, 1998.

Stern, David H. *The Jewish New Testament Commentary: A Companion Volume to the Jewish New Testament*. Clarksville, MD: Jewish New Testament Publications, 1992.

Tomlin, Graham. *The Provocative Church*. 3d ed. London: SPCK, 2009.

Among many others, here are a few churches in the Chicago area we learn from:

Canaan Community Church: www.canaancommunitychurch.org

Lawndale Community Church: www.lawndalechurch.org

Rock of Our Salvation Church: www.rockofoursalvation.com

REFLECTION

(In using the following sentence to guide your writing, be as specific as your can, even including some Scripture if you feel it is appropriate.)

Almighty God, when I envision about your Kingdom come on earth as it is in heaven, I see…

CHARACTERISTIC #5: THRIVING YOUTH AND FAMILIES
Creating a web of supportive friendships

In the last days, God says,
I will pour out my Spirit on all people.
Your sons and daughters will prophesy,
your young men will see visions,
your old men will dream dreams.

Acts 2:17

For in him we live and move and have our being.
As some of your own poets have said, "We are his offspring."

Acts 17:28

In the beginning was the Word, the manifest logic of God heard unblurred
shining from the inner sanctum of the third.
Unbroken catastrophical quotes spoken from the essence
of eternity's original notion.
All things were made by his motion and without him was no thing brought to
being—all matter engrossed him.
In him was life, and that life was the Light of men
shining in the dark, but darkness didn't comprehend.

John 1:1-5[10]

Hear, O Israel: The LORD our God, the LORD is one. Love the LORD your
God with all your heart and with all your soul and with all your strength.
These commandments I give you today are to be upon your hearts. Impress
them on your children. Talk about them when you sit at home and when you
walk along the road, when you lie down and when you get up. Tie them as
symbols on your hands and bind them on your foreheads. Write them on the
doorframes of your houses and on your gates.

Deuteronomy 6:4-9

---

10   Fred D. Lynch, *The Script: A Hip Hop Devotional through the Book of John* (Grand Rapids: Zondervan, 2008), 8.

by Melissa Ledbetter

In June 2012, Nate and I got to celebrate a milestone in our lives: ten years ago, we committed to grow a new branch of our families, to live our lives together, for the rest of our lives. Three years later, God continued to grow our family through adoption. He has added three more to us since then, through birth, directly into our family. And though we got here in different ways, this often-crazy "tribe," as we like to call it, this is us. We are family. We have so-much-fun times, we have painful times, we have you-make-me-laugh-so-hard times, we have I-can't-take-this-crazy-for-one-more-minute times, and we have a lot of I-love-you-so-much-I-can't-even-explain-it times. All of it makes up our life. And whether we are in the best of times or the worst of times, the thing that doesn't change is that we all belong.

The last few months of each year in our family mean a lot of birthdays, an adoption day, and then, for us all, the holidays. I've been thinking a lot about adoption this year—the true miracle of adoption. The miracle that means belonging at the very deepest level, that creates a true belonging that cannot be taken away. The miracle that with every word we speak about the beauty and significance of adoption in our family, we are also acknowledging the beauty and mystery of our belonging in Christ, in God's family.

I think a lot about how it all started, about how I get to be a part of this. Because, based on how it all began with Abraham and God's chosen people who came from him, based on the *natural* order of things, I really shouldn't even be talking about this, about belonging to the family of God. Not being of Jewish descent, if you go back to the whole idea of how being chosen got started, I wasn't. Yet God, in his love that I cannot begin to understand, made a way of adoption into

His family for those of us who didn't meet the original qualifications. And, amazingly, when belonging meant adherence to the law God gave through Moses, the heart of God even then was for his people to love and welcome the stranger.[11] As I live in this grace, which God has made available to everyone and is experienced by those who choose to follow the resurrected Christ, I find that in my humanity, my sense of belonging continues to grow stronger and deeper, and I take it less and less for granted.

I had a dream recently in which I was standing by a table that Jesus was preparing. The table extended so long that I couldn't see the end of it. As he prepared the table, I followed him around it, trying to get him to give me answers to all my questions (I had a lot). The only response he gave was, "There is enough room around the table for everyone who is supposed to be there." I stuck with him, asking more questions, trying desperately to communicate my deep need to know answers. All he said was, "There is enough."

I don't know who's often found around your table. I remember a few holiday dinners in my home growing up that included elderly people from our church who didn't have other family. I may not have even known some of their last names, but the spirit around the table was that they were invited, they were welcomed, and they belonged there with us. We have celebrated so many birthdays and holidays with people to whom we don't belong by birth, but who have let us and many others know over the years that we belong.

So, come on—let's be those who welcome. You're invited and you are wanted. And, in case you're wondering, there's enough room for everyone.

---

11   Deuteronomy 10:19.

THOUGHTS

What are the standards by which we are developing our youth?

Are we approaching relationships with youth holistically
(cognitive, social, emotional, physical, spiritual)?

Are we aware of the environments our youth are living within?

In what ways do our youth have access to life-giving social networks
and relational associations?

How are we teaching our youth to be people of character?

How are we demonstrating that same character in our own lives?

In what ways are the voices of youth being heard, gaining
opportunities to be homegrown leaders?

How are children and students able to play and thrive on the block?

Is our block a positive place for youth to grow up and flourish?

How do you see families growing together?

Are families and neighbors breaking bread and eating together
on a regular basis?

Are basic needs being met on the block, needs like food,
security, and monthly expenses?

How are parents connecting and being supportive
of each other?

Are marriages healthy and growing?
What are we doing to support this?

Do youth on the block have access to quality educational options?

How are parents and people on our block coming together to help
raise and educate children?

Are we tapped into today's technology, poets, musicians, artists, and
how our youth communicate? How so?

Are local neighbors guiding youth as a "village of mentors" among all
the children here?

Are there ways we can more effectively listen to our youth,
providing outlets for their leadership voices and
perspectives to be heard?

What are the neighborhood conditions that produce despair?

What symptoms are we noticing among youth that could
be linked to a larger cause or unjust system?

Are we seeing children and students as people of beauty, wonder, and
gifting? How are we embracing them as a gift among us?

Are we willing to learn from students as leaders at the table?
How can we better facilitate this?

How are we passing on the stories of God's faithfulness
to the next generation?

STARTING POINTS

By the Hand Kids Club is a Chicago-based after-school program that
continues to make incredible in roads throughout Chicago, especially
within the Austin neighborhood where about 180 youth come to
a center each day to receive spiritual care, love, and educational
mentoring to reach their potential. By the Hand emphasizes academic
excellence and nurtures the whole child—mind, body, and soul.

Passing on a vibrant faith to the next generation is a communal effort.
Notice to whom Deuteronomy 6:4-9 is addressed—the community
of Israel. As we seek to empower the next generation now, it will
take the entire community. Here are a few more places that can
offer us encouragement:

www.paladinyouthdevelopment.com
www.DVULI.org
www.Zone850.org/standards
www.holisticeducation.net
www.bythehand.org
www.skinnerleadership.org
www.newlifecdc.us (especially "Young Governors")
www.mercystreetdallas.org

www.pottershouseschool.org

www.daystarschool.com

www.HCZ.org

www.realresources.com

www.paultough.com

www.grassrootsgrantmakers.org (especially "A Conversation with John McKnight on The Abundant Community"—July 7, 2010)

Brueggemann, Walter. *Using God's Resources Wisely: Isaiah and Urban Possibility*. Louisville: Westminster John Knox, 1993.

Dyson, Michael Eric. *Know What I Mean?: Reflections on Hip-Hop*. New York: Basic Civitas Books, 2010.

ESV Urban Devotional Bible. Wheaton: Crossway Books, 2007.

Fountain, John W. *Dear Dad: Reflections on Fatherhood*. Chicago: WestSide Press, 2011.

Haugen, Gary A. *Just Courage: God's Great Expedition for the Restless Christian*. Downers Grove, IL: InterVarsity Press, 2008.

Schlabach, Joetta Handrich. *Extending the Table: Recipes and stories of people from Argentina to Zambia in the spirit of More-with-Less*. Scottsdale, PA: Herald Press, 1991.

Smith, Efrem. *Raising Up Young Heroes: Developing a Revolutionary Youth Ministry*. Downers Grove, IL: InterVarsity Press, 2004.

REFLECTION

Almighty God, when I think about the youth of our community, our (my) greatest burden for them is…

Our (my) greatest joy is…

Youth and students are expressing the following dreams and concerns…

CHARACTERISTIC #6: EMPOWERED ELDERS

Closing the gap between the younger and older

This is what the LORD says:
"Stand at the crossroads and look;
ask for the ancient paths,
ask where the good way is, and walk in it,
and you will find rest for your souls."
Jeremiah 6:16

Even when I am old and gray,
do not forsake me, O God,
till I declare your power to the next generation,
your might to all who are to come.
Psalm 71:18

One generation will commend your works to another;
they will tell of your mighty acts.
They will speak of the glorious splendor of your majesty,
and I will meditate on your wonderful works.
They will tell of the power of your awesome works,
and I will proclaim your great deeds.
Psalm 145:4-6

While I was away on a working trip with my friend, Leroy, our elderly neighbor next door, Miss Mary, called and left a voicemail on my mobile phone, "Hello, Nate, this is Miss Mary. I hope you're having a great trip. I wanted you to know that Melissa and the kids are all good. I stayed up all night long watching your home through the blinds of my window to be sure your family was safe last night. Have a good trip. Bring God with you and always bring him back."

Miss Mary always ended our conversations as a reminder to "bring God with me," which I experienced as a call to be aware of God's presence each day and everywhere.

I hung up the phone in awe. While my wife and children were sleeping soundly and while I was out of town, my elderly neighbor was pulling a college all-nighter to make sure our family was safe and well. We didn't ask for this kind of love. My wife wasn't in fear. We were going about our days and nights as normal, and yet our dear sister tangibly demonstrated the generous care, covering, and nurturing of God.

At her own expense, out of her own time and sacrifice as she felt led, she pulled an all-nighter on our behalf. She was re-neighboring her block, looking out for us in friendship and love. She could have gone to bed, but she chose to stay up out of love. She demonstrated in one night what takes a lifetime of practice to learn what it means to be a neighbor. Miss Mary inspires me, and I thank God for the way she spoke into our lives as extended family.

I'm convinced that a thriving city block demonstrates intergenerational friendships exchanging love and hospitality. Don't be distracted by the act of an all-nighter. Staying up all night isn't necessarily what we're meant to do. It's the heart, motive, spirit, character, and generosity that Miss Mary was willing to cultivate over the course of her life. Like Miss Mary, I pray that God will grow us into becoming good neighbors over a lifetime of practicing love, passing on the wonder of God to those who come behind us.

THOUGHTS

Are seniors able to thrive on this block or nearby?
What are the signs that this is happening?

What is the relationship like between local seniors
and the neighborhood? Between elderly parents
and their grown children?

Do seniors have the assistance they need from their
extended family and faith community?

Are people caring for widows here?

What are the concerns of our elderly?

What are their hopes and dreams?

What stories, lessons, or principles can we learn
from those who have gone before us?

Are seniors cared for and surrounded with positive friendships?
How do we see this happening?

Are there issues or concerns that our elderly want to discuss?
What are they?

Are there areas where our most vulnerable seniors are being taken
advantage of through scams or other oppressive systems?

Do our seniors have adequate heating and cooling?

How is the overall living condition of seniors on our block?

In what ways are the elders teaching the younger, and the younger
honoring the elderly?

How are we gleaning the wisdom of those who have gone ahead of us?

What knowledge can neighbors on the block teach to someone else?
How can we help facilitate this?

STARTING POINTS

Due to a dwindling economy, more and more seniors are living with
their families. Society needs more models, examples, and resources that
relate to the empowerment and dignity of our senior citizens. Many
of our elderly neighbors in The United States need trusted friends to
assist them with running errands, grocery shopping, medical assistance,
or simply by being present with no agenda other than enjoying each
other's company. To learn more, read "Top Ten Trends in Senior
Housing for 2013" by George Yedinak (http://seniorhousingnews.
com/2013/01/07/top-10-trends-in-senior-housing-for-2013/)

REFLECTION

Take some time to reflect with the elderly in your community.
What are your dreams? What brings you joy? What burdens you?
What is your lifestory?

Write down your thoughts in the form of a prayer to God.

CHARACTERISTIC #7:
MEANINGFUL WORK
AND OPPORTUNITY

Sometimes justice wears a suit

The LORD works righteousness
and justice for all the oppressed.
Psalm 103:6

He has shown you, O mortal, what is good.
And what does the Lord require of you?
To act justly and to love mercy
and to walk humbly with your God.
Micah 6:8

When the righteous prosper, the city rejoices;
when the wicked perish, there are shouts of joy.
Proverbs 11:10[12]

For you yourselves know how you ought to follow our example. We were not
idle when we were with you, nor did we eat anyone's bread without paying
for it. On the contrary, we worked night and day, laboring and toiling so that
we would not be a burden to any of you.
2 Thessalonians 3:7-8

---

12   For a beautiful exploration of the word "righteous" and a theological framework
of the Hebrew word *tsaddiqim*, see Amy L. Sherman, *Kingdom Calling: Vocational*
Stewardship for the Common Good (Downers Grove, IL:
InterVarsity Press, 2011).

When our family was visiting with Miss Lillie in her living room, we heard men yelling outside. Miss Lillie asked me, "Nate, what's all that commotion outside?" We concluded it was probably the house across the street. At the risk of reinforcing stereotypes or fears about under-resourced neighborhoods, "commotion" is not a 24/7 experience, but it was frequently the reality of our city block.

And so, knowing my wife, Melissa, was out front working in Miss Lillie's flowerbed, we walked outside to see what all the fuss was about. Two men were standing their ground in each other's faces and emotions were running high. Unlike other times during similar situations, I sensed the Spirit of God directing me to walk quietly toward the street. Melissa and Miss Lillie stood behind me on the front porch. I walked slowly and didn't say a word. I just watched and prayed. I wanted the guys to know that enough was enough. Eyes are on the street.

Eventually, the two men saw us and decided to part ways calmly. In that split second, I thought, "Oh, thank you, God; all is well," until one of the guys came barreling toward me. In no time, I experienced a strong sense of the brevity of life. He threatened to shoot me while my wife's "mother bear" came out in the form of hollering behind me, "Excuse me?!? Yeah, I'm talking to you!" (For the record, no one messes with my wife.) And so I stood my ground, not as some kind of hero, but as a man knowing my wife could take anyone. Okay, seriously. This was not looking good. What had I done? All I knew was to stand.

Until the Spirit of God seemingly took over in the moment, giving me the words to speak, "Listen, all I'm doing is standing here praying for peace! *Peace*! That's all I want is *peace*. I'm praying for *peace*!" The man responded with a pause, "You're praying?" We both stared at each other in disbelief. "Yes," I said. "I'm praying for peace." To which the man said, "Okay." And he walked away.

Meanwhile, Miss Lillie shook her head and we all chuckled a little with heavy hearts for a hurting man who needs the kind of healing that only comes from God through the hope of knowing and following Jesus. The kind of hope that I know I need. And then about five minutes later, the man got into his car and rolled up in front of my house. He stepped out of the driver's side door and apologized in front of our entire city block, "I apologize. I shouldn't have said what I did." This was a moment I will never forget for the rest of my life. "Apology accepted. Although, when you threaten a man's life, I'm trying to determine if I need to call the police or not. Are we good?" As the block looked on from a distance, he answered, "Yeah, we're good." And in that moment, I realized how God seemed to be opening my heart toward this man, and it seemed his heart was open toward mine.

To be clear, this man marked me in a positive way. He is the courageous one in the story. Perhaps we called out the courage in each other, but he was the one who walked away from a fight with my other neighbor. And after hearing me out, he chose to walk away from me without imposing an act of violence. And finally, he did what real men do. He made a public apology, owned up to his mistake, and chose to name what he had done in front of other neighbors on our block. I salute this man's courage and character.

And quite honestly, we as a society need to create other positive, viable options for meaningful work and opportunity. A lack of jobs combined with generational poverty, fatherlessness,[13] oppressive spiritual

---

13   According to the US Census Bureau, 24 million children in the United States —one out of three—live in biological father-absent homes. See more at http://www. fatherhood.org/media/consequences-of-father-absence-statistics.

strongholds, and the stress of surviving the streets only intensifies the evil hold of pathological violence among younger men.[14] This goes beyond the scope of the United States. I will always remember the moment when a few pastors in the underground church of North Africa asked me to pray for jobs. The need for dignified work to support families is everywhere.

We need more men from all walks of life to step up. We need strong peacemakers with a clear sense of identity to choose life over death and courage over fear. Are we paying attention to the power of words in our lives? Are we aware of the effect we have on each other? How are we thinking about future generations and our responsibility to instill the character of God's goodness? How does God's goodness translate into real life among those who often lack access to living wage jobs, training, and guidance?

I continue to pray for peace. I feel challenged by the words of Jesus, "Blessed are the peacemakers," and I am challenged by the principles of nonviolence that Dr. King often spoke about. He chose peace with a relentless fortitude, even after his house was bombed and his family was continually threatened.

Late that night I prayed, *"God, help me. I want to be a peacemaker in a world of violence."*

---

14   On spiritual strongholds and the condition of our hearts: What causes a lack of access to resources and opportunities is central to this conversation. Our systems are broken. And a lack of neighboring friendships gives room for fear, and fear often propels the conditions that produce despair. May God give us the nerve to live freely and courageously. Check out the following website related to Michelle Alexander's book, "The New Jim Crow: Mass Incarceration in the Age of Colorblindness." www.newjimcrow.com

THOUGHTS

What is the history of business in our neighborhood or community?

Who were some of the original entrepreneurs and store-owners?

Where were those businesses originally located?

Is there a local business network?

Who owns the real estate here?

How can we most meaningfully fight poverty by strengthening
local businesses here?

What are people dreaming about and how is the level of
entrepreneurial energy in the neighborhood?

How is the business environment here for the next generation?

Where are the local business assets to build upon?

How might we consider "co-investing" our lives with local
entrepreneurs through an exchange of time, resources,
and friendship?

Do local business owners and aspiring entrepreneurs have access to
adequate technology, positive working environments, printing
resources, and business coaching?

How can we draw upon each other's gifts in the midst
of our business deserts?

Is business on the block a re-investment within the community
(recycling the local dollar)?

Are local people making the first investment with skin in the game?

Are local shop owners providing quality goods and services
with a positive presence?

Are businesses and companies partnering with the local neighborhood,
creating sustainable job options to support families?
How many?

Are business professionals engaged within the community—
stewarding skills, resources, connections, and know-how—for
justice's sake and with God's heart in mind?

Do families live simply and generously with a healthy respect for
money and stewardship?

Is there a strong community work ethic with meaningful, productive
work made available? Is this productive work accessible
to the community?

What are the assets of this place?

Who are the producers?

Where are people giving wisely and with sustainable "energy"?[15]

---

15   For a fuller discussion of this concept, see Robert D. Lupton, *Toxic Charity:
How Churches and Charities Hurt Those They Help (And How to Reverse It)* (New York:
HarperOne, 2011), 117.

STARTING POINTS

While serving years ago as a pastor at Mars Hill Bible Church in West Michigan, I discovered that many professionals do not mind swinging a hammer, but they would rather offer their professional expertise in ways that build God's economy. Consider inviting professionals to see themselves as "vocational neighbors" through business and job creation (see Glossary of Common Terms and the Epilogue).

Sunshine Gospel Enterprises is currently developing a phenomenal model for business engagement and job creation in Chicago, Illinois. Learn more at www.sunshinegospel.org

Developing opportunities for meaningful work requires partnership across a broad spectrum, to that end, here are a few websites and resources that could be helpful in your context:

www.urbanonramps.com
www.vocationalstewardship.org
www.partnersworldwide.org
www.bethelnewlife.org
www.launchchattanooga.org
www.opportunitynicaragua.org
www.jobsforlife.org
www.ccda.org (especially the Future Profits Curriculum)
www.faithandwork.org
www.barnabasgroup.org
www.metromerge.org
www.kingdombusinessuniversity.com
www.fcsministries.org (especially "Pride for Parents")
www.freshharvestdelivered.com
www.bamthinktank.org

www.chalmers.org

www.generousgiving.org

www.kingdomadvisors.org

www.risingtidecapital.org

www.bankofideas.com.au

www.exploradelphia.com

www.ssireview.org

www.acumen.org/ten (especially "Ten Things We've Learned About Tackling Global Poverty")

www.communitiesfirstassociation.org

Fisman, Raymond, Rakesh Khurana, and Edward Martenson. "Mission-Driven Governance." *Stanford Social Innovation Review Vol. 7, No. 3* (Summer 2009).

Galvin, James C. "Strategic Plans That Learn: An Innovative Alternative to Traditional Strategic Planning." *Outcomes Magazine* (Summer 2010): 20-2.

Green, Gary, Anna Haines, and Stephen Halebsky. *Building Our Future: A Guide to Community Visioning*. Madison, WI: Cooperative Extension Publications, 2000.

Hanleybrown, Fay, John Kania, and Mark Kramer. "Channeling Change: Making Collective Impact Work." No pages. Cited 26 January 2012. Online: http://www.ssireview.org/blog/entry/channeling_change_making_collective_impact_work.

Lowney, Chris. *Heroic Leadership: Best Practices from a 450-Year-Old Company That Changed the World*. Chicago: Loyola Press, 2005.

Metzger, Michael. *Sequencing: Deciphering Your Company's DNA.* Waukesha: Game Changer Books, 2010.

Nelson, Mary. *Empowerment: A Key Component of Christian Community Development.* Bloomington, IN: iUniverse, 2010.

Rickett, Daniel. *Making Your Partnership Work: A Guide for Ministry Leaders.* Enumclaw, WA: WinePress Publishing, 2002.

"Money and Power" by Oscar Muriu (http://www.youtube.com/watch?v=XmghXX41afU)

REFLECTION

Almighty God, you have given us hands to work—work that gives us meaning, dignity, and a sense of productivity. When we create and work, we are following in your footsteps, for you are the Master Creator. Together, with my neighbors, our dream for our community is…

CHARACTERISTIC #8: QUALITY HOUSING

*Creating healthy, sustainable
living for everyone*

Justice will dwell in the desert
and righteousness will live in the fertile field.
The fruit of that righteousness will be peace;
its effect of righteousness will be quietness and confidence forever.
My people will live in peaceful dwelling places,
in secure homes,
in undisturbed places of rest.
Though hail flattens the forest
and the city is leveled completely,
how blessed will you be,
sowing your seed by every stream,
and letting your cattle and donkeys range free.

Isaiah 32:16-20

Unless the LORD builds the house,
its builders labor in vain.
Unless the LORD watches over the city,
the watchmen stand guard in vain.
In vain you rise early
and stay up late,
toiling for food to eat—
for he grants sleep to those he loves.

Psalm 127:1-2

In 2008, Melissa and I co-directed the staff of Charis Community Housing (CCH) in Atlanta, Georgia. CCH is the housing ministry partner of FCS Urban Ministries. Bob Lupton, the Founder and President of FCS, asked us to consider serving as co-executive directors of CCH to fill a temporary leadership void for a short season. I chuckled a little at first because I thought Bob was joking. It turned out he was serious. I was thirty-years-old at the time and my vocational experience had been serving in a formal pastoral role prior to moving to Atlanta. Melissa and I knew very little about housing, but we were passionate about the need for quality housing in our community. Under Bob's mentorship, we agreed to lead the organization temporarily as interim directors until hiring our long-term replacement later that year.

As many of us remember, 2008 was a tough year as the economic bubble in the United States began to burst. Housing sales plummeted as cities across the nation experienced foreclosures. The cost of construction supplies began to rise and banks began to offload thousands of homes into regional portfolios. The idea of purchasing one home within one particular neighborhood for concentrated impact became much more challenging. The entire industry was changing all at once. In some ways, realtors were re-learning their profession as the foreclosure landscape became the new norm. Even long-term housing experts became students again. Non-profit leaders, realtors, bankers, pastors, business people, contractors, and civic leaders were all attempting to understand what was happening together.

At the time, CCH had a reputation for new housing construction, but now, empty foreclosed homes built on mortgage fraud and erroneous information were scattered throughout our neighborhood. Perhaps what some meant for mortgage fraud, God meant for good. I remember when our neighbor only had three days to find a place to live because her landlord never told her that the home she rented was being foreclosed. And so we joined Bob and the rest of the board to guide a team process to secure funding, stop the bleeding, and stabilize the housing crises in our neighborhood. Together, we decided to stop all new construction. Marketplace minds rallied together to create a "Foreclosure Redemption Strategy" that aligned with the neighborhood's housing master plan to protect the vulnerable, ensure quality housing, and avoid re-concentrating pockets of poverty or wealth. While funding remains tight, Charis continues to make headway.

No matter where we find ourselves, our place of living has a significant impact on our lives. Homes and apartments are places where children are meant to grow up with a secure sense of guidance and wonder. Jesus often entered the homes of many where he experienced the intimacy of sharing a meal to talk about life. And with home as a central contributor to the health of families, there are many among us who survive each month with hope for a stable home: underemployed immigrants who work low-wage jobs, refugees from war-torn countries, and many other neighbors who grow up in the cycle of generational poverty.

As a starting point, together we commit to:

- Dedicate our own home as a place of peace, as a lighthouse and refuge on the block.
- Work with neighbors to express God's love through the redemptive swing of a hammer.
- Honor the history, culture, story, and local architecture of the neighborhood.
- Raise quality control in the way we build or rehab homes over a "quick flip."
- Reduce our carbon footprint through construction that benefits the next generation.
- Use open-slatted fences over privacy fences to promote neighboring and safety.
- Use open glass security doors and windows over bars and barricades.
- Stand with those who are vulnerable to secure policy and practice with integrity.
- Recruit integrity-filled landlords who rent and manage properties with dignity.
- Co-invest with neighbors in ways that move people toward empowerment.

THOUGHTS

Is quality housing accessible, affordable, and sustainable on the block?

Is there a neighborhood housing master plan in place to protect the
vulnerable, ensuring a place of living for all people?

Are grassroots voices sitting at the decision-making table? If not, how
can we ensure they are?

What is the percentage of homeowners and renters
within the community?

What do local neighbors desire?

Is the surrounding housing market healthy and mixed-income,
inviting neighbors to cross over barriers of isolation
(vs. re-concentrating pockets of poverty and wealth)?

How are neighbors, churches, and businesses stewarding land and real
estate in partnership with the neighborhood?

What is the nature of our city housing policies and procedures?

Are landowners, homeowners, and renters caring for homes with
responsibility, quality control, and excellence?

Are homes and apartments built well with sustainable practices that
honor generations to come (e.g. green insulation, tankless
water heaters, low flow toilets)?

Is the economy stagnant or in motion? What are the signs of this?

Is the community able to sustain quality business
and homes in the area?

Is disposable income increasing to create local marketplaces, farmers
markets, grocery stores, or other crucial elements that overlap
with quality housing?

How are we caring for our friends who are without
a home in this place?

How are we creatively advocating for others here?

Who are the community connectors here?

Are their local banks and investors here?

What new or proven practices need to be applied to ensure
quality housing in this city?

Who is already doing great work in this area and how can
we work together?

STARTING POINTS

Quality housing is an essential ingredient for the presence of dignity in a neighborhood. A lack of quality housing keeps a neighborhood enslaved to negative patterns that work against esteem, justice, and dignity. The following are some places where you can explore some different housing models for neighborhoods:

www.chariscommunity.org
www.ehresmanmanagement.com
www.fullercenter.org
www.makinghousinghappen.net
www.NW.org
www.perpetualhelphome.org
www.urbanhomeworks.org
www.waltoncommunities.com

REFLECTION

As we process through the issue of quality housing in our neighborhood context, let's create two lists—one with words or phrases that describe a community that is striving for quality housing, and a second list with words or phrases that describe a community without access to quality housing. What do we learn from these lists? How might our perspective be limited? Who else can we learn with or from to broaden our perspective?

Almighty God, our dream for our community when it comes to housing is…

CHARACTERISTIC #9:
QUALITY OF LIFE

Pursuing integrity in all aspects of life

By night I went out through the Valley Gate toward the Jackal
Well and the Dung Gate, examining the walls of Jerusalem, which
had been broken down, and its gates, which had been destroyed by fire.
Nehemiah 2:13[16]

I will walk about in freedom,
for I have sought out your precepts.
I will speak of your statutes before kings
and will not be put to shame,
for I delight in your commands
because I love them.
I will lift up my hands to your commands, which I love,
that I may meditate on your decrees.
Psalm 119:45-48

---

16   You might also want to reflect upon Exodus 1, Acts 15, and the books of Ezra
and Nehemiah as a holistic perspective on rebuilding communities.

The old brick building on the corner of our block seemed to tell a story. It was almost as if it had a voice of its own, inviting others to hear the narrative of neighborhood history and perseverance. It was a beautiful building. It was known as one of the original storefront businesses that originally included a small grocery store and barbershop. I suppose a lack of care for the building, along with the natural effects of the weather, combined with a strong need to preserve the tuck points between the bricks eventually gave way to its disintegration. Brick-by-brick, the building gave way to gravity as the walls and windows began to bend over time.

On the side of the building, youth tagged the wall with graffiti, "R.I.P. Eli," and the flimsy boards over the windows seemed to invite trouble. Eventually, the roof caved in and the sunlight beamed through hidden angles of history. It seemed as though it was just a matter of time before the city would take care of the matter. Neighbors often expressed a strong desire for the building to be torn down. It was a real safety concern. Several neighbors used to pray over the building and all around the space for protection over youth and children who walked near the building during many hours of the day and night. The building reminded me daily that the need for quality of life is essential for the peace and presence of God to flourish on my block.

Neighbors eventually rallied to voice concern, calling the city, offering photos of building code violations, demanding that something be done soon, even now. While we understood that there are many other buildings with code violations, this particular storefront was a unique danger zone on a busy corridor. The property owner was simply nowhere to be found with no accountability. We needed a response. We needed action, but we didn't have a strong enough collective voice.

And then one evening, as I was driving home after a hard summer rainstorm, I noticed the crowd gathering around the corner of our block. Police were re-directing traffic while city personnel tore down the remaining bricks. It was sad because, despite its flaws, we loved that building. But lightening had struck the top wall and the city had no choice but to finish the job. The remaining challenge was that the city didn't remove the rubble. They simply tore down the bricks and left a large pile where the storefront once stood tall. In the following months, the city claimed they didn't tear the building down and that it must have been someone else. After neighbors sent pictures of the city vehicles from that evening, the city agreed to come back to clean up the rubble, but it took the effort of neighbors calling on a regular basis to get the job done.

For many of us, this is just one example of many situations that exist around the country. Empty houses and storefronts left by absentee landlords, and carte blanche zoning permissions allow industrial businesses, tow yards, and landfills to congregate within under-resourced neighborhoods. Environmental racism is real. We need partnerships with others who will seek to understand the challenges and lend their voices beside ours to create wholesome places for children. So that in the midst of global crises and the pain of broken systems, there is a joy-filled, more hopeful picture that the Spirit is painting.

Beauty is external in things we can see with our physical eyes, but it is also found where we can see through the eyes of our hearts, where we can see that God is still on the move in our streets, around our dinner tables and front porches.

Somehow the struggle is a catalyst to reveal and refine the beauty that already surrounds us. Some of my mistreated, dismissed neighbors are the friends teaching me most about life and generosity, faith and forgiveness. In this way, the Spirit is regenerating life in small places, in hidden, devastated corners of our global cities. And so we press on.

It's a beautiful thing.

THOUGHTS

What are the assets and gifts here that neighbors are building upon?

How is the relationship between neighbors and public service officials?

Are city services efficient and excellent (clean water, accessible transportation, emergency response, trash, and recycling)?

Is the street vibrant with life, light, and presence? What are the signs of this happening?

Do most neighbors consider the surrounding area safe and walkable?

How are neighbors experiencing the surrounding environment?

Is there a need for increased density, short cross walks, wide pathways, bikeways, adequate lighting, LED lights, or more green space and parks? What can be done about this need?

Are sidewalks, streets, and plazas designed with beauty and community in mind?

Is there a need for more trees, flowers, or traffic calming street designs?

Are there zoning challenges here?

What trends are we noticing throughout the surrounding
blocks in the area?

Are buildings, land, and spaces being built, renovated, or maintained in
stewardship of our "environmental footprint?" How so?

How is the overall health of children and families in the local area?

Is the area one of peace and wholeness? Is our city block
welcoming and hospitable to all?

How will we advocate with others to join the winds of change?

STARTING POINTS

Encouraging a deeper quality of life is all about opportunities—
opportunities to be safe, affirm dignity, and experience beauty
and justice. It is about our physical surroundings, but also about
our interior life. As you investigate the quality of life in your
neighborhood, here are a few places to begin the discussion:

www.bethelnewlife.org
www.urbanophile.com
www.theblackurbanist.com
www.archpaper.com
www.nextcity.org

www.theatlanticcities.com

www.streetsblog.org

www.flourishonline.org (especially see "livability, walkability, and environmental justice" resources and "walkability checklist")

www.CNU.org

www.newurbanism.org (while principles of new urbanism are applicable, we must be aware of social, economic, and racial implications as they relate to gentrification, power, and white privilege)

www.growingpower.org

www.sweetwater-organic.com

www.GACM.org

Jacobs, Jane. *The Death and Life of Great American Cities*. 50th Anniversary Edition. New York: Modern Library, 2011.

Jacobsen, Eric O. *Sidewalks in the Kingdom: New Urbanism and the Christian Faith*. Grand Rapids: Brazos, 2003.

_____. *The Space Between: A Christian Engagement With The Built Environment*. Grand Rapids: Baker Academic, 2012.

Kretzmann, John P., and John L. McKnight. *Building Communities From the Inside Out: A Path Toward Finding And Mobilizing A Community's Assets*. Chicago: ACTA Publishing, 1993.

The New York City Department of Transportation published a *Street Design Manual* in 2009. Originally written to "[build] on the experience of innovation in street design, materials, and lighting that has developed around the world," NYC is committed to share continued updates to the manual that reflect streets designed for safety, access and mobility, context, livability, and sustainability. To learn more, visit www.NYC.gov/dot.

REFLECTION

Almighty God, when I close my eyes and think about what our community *could* be, I…

CHARACTERISTIC #10:
CREATIVE PURPOSE
Imagining and working together

For we are the product of His hand, heaven's poetry etched on lives, *created in the Anointed, Jesus, to accomplish the good works God arranged long ago.*

Ephesians 2:10 (The Voice)

Now to him who is able to do immeasurably more than all we ask or imagine, according to his power that is at work within us, to him be glory in the church and in Christ Jesus throughout all generations, for ever and ever! Amen.

Ephesians 3:20-21

One thing I ask from the LORD,
this is what I seek:
that I may dwell in the house of the LORD
all the days of my life,
to gaze on the beauty of the LORD
and to seek him in his temple.

Psalm 27:4

Can you fathom the mysteries of God?
Can you probe the limits of the Almighty?
They are higher than the heavens—what can you do?
They are deeper than the depths of the grave—what can you know?
Their measure is longer than the earth
and wider than the sea.

Job 11:7-9

David, ceremonially dressed in priest's linen,
danced with great abandon before GOD.

2 Samuel 6:14 (MSG)

A friend of mine happens to be an international graffiti artist. His work commands respect. We met a few years back after "the big search" when I decided I *had* to meet the man, the legend who prefers to stay under the radar. For months I kept searching, asking folks all around the city, "Who painted that?"

After another mad search, a friend of mine pointed me to his website and I finally was able to get ahold of him. I quickly learned that this guy is a man of integrity and candidness, and his way of engaging people while being fully himself is marking my life to this day. I'm grateful for the way God is changing me through his commitment to listening and truth telling. The first project we worked on together was a set of small murals in our neighborhood that eventually led to other larger projects, and the pure fun of those initial moments seemed to ignite a process of imagination between us. We soon found ourselves exchanging ideas and views on life, sensing that this was the beginning of a new partnership.

Artists whose names we may never know create in lots of ways all around us, prophetically calling us to think about reality from different vantage points. Varied forms of public art—murals, sculptures, graffiti, music, design, dance, and much more—offer cultural insights, hope, and healing in society.

Artists young and old tap into a practical imagination that God intends to draw out of communities. God's glory is wide and high, but it also runs deep—right here on the ground where you can taste and see beauty in the streets. Maybe God's glory is gritty, bearing witness through the imagination of people partnering together. We might call this "interdependent imagination." What really draws my attention is engaging the process in real time, listening to people's thoughts and dreams as neighbors lead the way.

Creativity is a God-given imprint of the Divine upon us. We see the nature of God's image through the hands of human beings who create, design, think, imagine, sew, explore, weave, and wonder. Around the world, we notice the bright and bold expressions of our clothing and cultures, potteries and projects. We truly are the "*artwork of God*" as stated in the book of Ephesians, "*made in advance for good works.*" And like anything in life, if we're not attentive to our motives, our God-given creativity can end up hijacked by something a little ugly. Some of us are in danger of becoming isolated behind the safety of our laptops. We're in danger of creating something that points back to ourselves, for own benefit, rather than creating *with* our neighbors to express the essence of God's joy in the neighborhood.

The following is a short list of two primary ways of creating. The left column describes the danger of creative narcissism. The right column describes a way of creating with others.

CULTURE OF COOL	GOD'S ENDLESS CREATIVITY
Seeks to be original	Seeks to join others with open hands
Attempts to make a statement	Attempts to build others up, inviting us toward God's heart for all people, especially those who suffer
Is a call to follow me or us	Speaks as a call to live beyond ourselves
Focuses on making a name	Focuses on carrying the Name well
Limited to a particular project or organization	Has no limits or boundaries
Focuses on drawing attention to ourselves	Focuses on generously giving credit
Has a limited, inward mindset	Promotes diversity, unity, & oneness
Isolated, homogenous, restricted, and irrelevant	In rhythm with neighbors through open imagination and diverse artistic expression
Comes from the strain of our own efforts	Comes from the Spirit of God
Found as individuals	Found in the context of community
Seeks to be like the surrounding culture	Seeks to engage and lead culture forward
Moves to a point of stagnant replication	In motion, adaptive, and innovative

There is a fine line in the creative process between these two ways, but the work toward endless creativity is worth the risk. Why are we doing this? Who is this for? What's at stake? I believe the fullness of our creativity is reserved in the space where people who are unlike each other come together. Until that happens, we're simply limiting the scope, wonder, and joy of God's endless creativity. Imagine that.

THOUGHTS

Where do we sense the movement of God on our block?
          What does it look like?

Where do we see signs of life or beauty on our
          street or in our community?

How often are people dreaming of the "what if" questions?

Are people free to imagine with hope and dignity?

Do youth have opportunities to cultivate their gifts and passions?

Are neighbors celebrating life through fiestas, murals, music, dance,
          poetry, redemptive graffiti, spoken word, cultural traditions,
          or other forms of art?

Do local murals reflect what local neighbors desire and hope
          for within the community?

What are the public spaces like? Is there public furniture available—
things like benches, bike racks, bus stop shelters, public
toilets, and more?

If yes, are they designed with creativity and in a way that
honors the dignity of all people?

Is imagination with purpose being fostered?

Are we dreaming big here?

Is there access to excellent gathering spaces and social
outlets for all to enjoy?

How does architecture contribute to history, culture, and local
innovation in this place?

What new and bold things are we yet to find, create, or build upon?

What needs to be reclaimed or repurposed?

How can we express the love of God here?

Who are the artists, visionaries, and creators here?

Where do we need to explore a little more?

What are the fears or the voices holding us back?

Are we open to new possibilities—even when it hurts?
Do we dare to dream once more?

STARTING POINTS

Check out The Fire House Community Arts Center in Chicago. It's a new kind of "gym" for students who share interests outside of sports such as culinary arts, video editing, photography, recording, music, and dance (thafirehouse.org).

Dreaming is best done in the context of community. If you have not done so recently, gather some of the people in your community together for the sole purpose of dreaming—dreaming big. Hopefully, the following resource can provide some ideas or language to your dreams:

www.thahouse.org

www.inhabitconference.com

www.startwithwhy.com

www.plywoodpeople.com

www.theideacamp.ning.com

www.qideas.org

www.christianitytoday.com/thisisourcity

www.tuck.dartmouth.edu/people/vg

Brueggemann, Walter. *The Prophetic Imagination*. 2d ed. Minneapolis: Fortress Press, 2001.

Gilliam, Alex. "Building Blocks: What LEGOs can teach us about rebuilding cities." No pages. Cited 26 February 2012. Online: http://grist.org/cities/building-blocks-what-legos-teach-us-about-rebuilding-cities/.

Linkner, Josh. *Disciplined Dreaming: A Proven System to Drive Breakthrough Creativity*. San Francisco: Jossey-Bass, 2011.

Shinabarger, Jeff. *More or Less: Choosing a Lifestyle of Excessive Generosity*. Colorado Springs: David C. Cook, 2013.

Wilson Jr., Paul. *Dream B.I.G. in 3D: How to Pursue a Bold, Innovative, God-Inspired Life!* Kennesaw: ParaMind, 2009.

REFLECTION

In the next week or so, take some extended time to be alone.
Perhaps you want to revisit the ten characteristics of thriving city
blocks. During your time, allow the Spirit of God to direct and guide
your thoughts and dreams. What does your community look like?
What could it look like? What if?

EPILOGUE: HOW TO SPARK AN UPRISING

Now, maybe more than ever, many churches are positioned to re-imagine what church could be among people from many walks and cultures. The question is whether we are willing to take the risk or not. Sadly, however, many churches in the city are still operating in isolation and within themselves. Without a clear understanding of healthy exchange, mutual listening, and partnership among vulnerable communities in the city where pockets of poverty run deep, churches run the risk of becoming inconsequential to the movement of God's Kingdom.

Over the years, I have seen the fruit that comes from homogenous relationships—a feeling of isolation and a limiting of the potential of God's Kingdom. I have also experienced the redemptive impact of relationships built across race and class lines. While living within under-resourced neighborhoods, I have seen firsthand the devastating effect of real challenges—both personal and systemic—among people from many walks of life. Whether we recognize it or not, we are deeply connected to one another.

Justice, I am finding, is advocating for others with a righteous dissemination of power and stewardship. At the core, I believe the essence of biblical justice is being in right relationship with God, self, others, and creation. Justice is married to relationship, while injustice is divorced from relationship. Justice is grounded in the character of God and should thus be expressed in the character of God's people. Justice is the pursuit of wholeness and restoration—a restoration of relationship as God originally intended. As you seek biblical justice, the following suggestions might be useful in shaping the direction of your neighborhood involvement.

IDENTIFY YOUR ROLE WITH OTHERS ON MISSION

As I step back and observe what is happening within me and around me, I'm continually re-learning how the gospel renovates hearts and restores communities. The good news of Jesus is a calling to love and enjoy God forever as an outpouring of our love for neighbor. To love at all, we need to understand first who we are because the practice of understanding our identity on mission is crucial not only to our effectiveness, but also to our truthfulness. The truth is that we are meant to demonstrate our love for one another. And I really believe we can because Christ clearly taught us how and promised to empower us to do it.

To help us understand our identity on mission, here are three common communities I have observed that need each other while loving their neighbors. We'll explore some meaningful action steps and points of caution with each of them.

PARISH COMMUNITIES: A PEOPLE FOCUSED ON LOVING A DEFINED GEOGRAPHIC AREA.

A parish community roots itself in a place with clear boundaries. Local living is crucial to a people's mission, and the parish model seeks to harness concentrated energy, relationships, and resources block-by-block within its defined bounds. In this way it is similar to many historic expressions of Christianity, loving everyone within the parish lines, regardless of race, ethnicity, gender, or religion. A parish seeks to become family with those they live and work beside ("with and of" the community). As an expression of the new family Jesus came to establish ("Jew and Gentile"), a parish becomes a Christ-centered beloved community. Everyone and everything is ultimately intended to bring God glory—every child, senior, house, and blade of grass—everything is offered to God.

With regard to mission, parish communities cultivate friendships and holistic initiatives that weave the peace and presence of Christ among neighbors. Land and love are intertwined. With caution, sometimes vocational or collective partnerships are needed to assist a parish community by generating access to connections and resources, or by expanding one's tunnel focus with imagination and the expansiveness of God.

VOCATIONAL COMMUNITIES: A PEOPLE FOCUSED ON STEWARDING SKILLS, EXPERTISE, CONTACTS, AND RESOURCES.

A vocational community partners with others through meaningful work to increase capacity, flexibility, and sustainability. Vocational communities often take the form of a team of professionals, a company, a not-for-profit, or anyone seeking to redeem work life as an opportunity to be a neighbor—a vocational neighbor. Others come together at the grassroots level as artists, teachers, entrepreneurs, a taskforce, board of directors, or a cohort to work on a short-term project or long-term cause. Vocational communities also assist each other in identifying and igniting calling—the fire within. Typically life-long students, designers, artists, cultural architects, business professionals, philanthropists, CEOs, community developers, nonprofit leaders, and skilled laborers are drawn to vocational communities for a time, increasing access to expertise, know-how, and networks for the common good.

With regard to mission, vocational communities come alive as they listen, reflect, and create in community. Vocational communities focus on business-as-mission that often results in creating jobs, strengthening businesses, or forming expressions of art to promote social innovation while inspiring people toward their God-given purpose. With caution, sometimes parish or collective voices are needed to remind a vocational community to slow down, and they can introduce local people of peace who have been there for years, paving the way.

COLLECTIVE COMMUNITIES: A PEOPLE FOCUSED ON A WIDE-REACHING CALL TO ACTION THAT INSPIRES, CONNECTS, OR EQUIPS.

A collective community seeks to inspire, equip, and link people across geographic lines while bridging different worlds in some unique way. Although often rooted locally, a collective community has a wide reach, forming friendships between neighborhoods, cities, regions, cultures, or countries to accomplish a goal or purpose. This kind of expression engages a broad spectrum of Kingdom communities, including underground church movements throughout the world, commuter churches in the West, worship gatherings, summer camps, associations, affiliations, networks, intermediaries, city groups, and missional movements. A collective often invites people who are unlike each other into unity. The collective voice is ever expanding and pursues diversity in all sorts of ways, from gender to ethnicity, from age to economics, energetically calling upon others to join God's renewal in the world.

With regard to mission, collective communities are able to bring people together who seldom relate. A healthy collective welcomes people at the fringe of society, showing them the loving face of Jesus. Collectives are often able to engage people, raise awareness, and generate resources to expand a vision. With caution, sometimes parish or vocational voices are needed to remind a collective to wait and listen alongside local partners, remembering that the winds of change take time and that God does the changing.

IT TAKES ALL THREE

Looking over these three communities one thing becomes apparent. It takes all three kinds of communities for *Thriving City Blocks* to become a reality where we live, work, and worship. Each community has a unique calling and personality, so we need to remember to ask ourselves, What are people's fears and what is holding us back? What is at stake? Who has gone ahead and how can we partner together to strengthen the effort? What are the spiritual implications for all of us? How can we stand together? What questions do we need to ask[17]?

The writer of 1 Corinthians reminds us:

If the whole body were an eye, where would the sense of hearing be? If the whole body were an ear, where would the sense of smell be? … The eye cannot say to the hand, "I don't need you!" And the head cannot say to the

17   As you think about these questions, these Scriptures are truly amazing when it comes to partnership, equality, and the nature of giving and receiving: 2 Corinthians 8:13-15, 2 Corinthians 9, Psalm 112, and Philippians 4. Also, check out www.generousgiving.org, Daniel Rickett's practical book *Making Your Partnership Work: A Guide for Ministry Leaders*, and *Linking Arms, Linking Lives: How Urban-Suburban Partnerships Can Transform Communities* by Ronald Sider, John Perkins, Wayne Gordon, and F. Albert Tizon.

feet, "I don't need you!" On the contrary, those parts of the body that seem to be weaker are indispensable, and the parts that we think are less honorable we treat with special honor. . . . If one part suffers, every part suffers with it; if one part is honored, every part rejoices with it.[18]

EMBRACE THE WHOLE GOSPEL
FOR THE WHOLE NEIGHBORHOOD

Spiritual, social, and economic rebirth happens when we display the hopeful way of Jesus Christ, showing how the brilliance of God's Kingdom transforms everything—our relationships with God, with others, and with creation. This is the big picture of the Gospel. I believe that we are called to bring the whole Gospel—in all its complexity—to the whole neighborhood. Consider focusing your efforts in small geographic areas in partnership with local neighbors. Leverage your resources, channeling your collective impact.

The hopeful way of Jesus compels us to love God and to love our neighborhood as ourselves. We believe God wants to restore the brokenness of all things through the person of Jesus Christ—our relationships with God, self, others and creation. We embrace the suffering of Christ, daily carrying our own crosses. We believe the tomb is empty, and we want to practice resurrection in the way we live and work. And so we trust the whole gospel to meet the needs of a whole neighborhood, including all of who we are as mind, body, soul, and emotion as well as the spiritual, social, and economic fabric of our neighborhoods.

And in our brokenness, God is changing us.

18   1 Corinthians 12:17-26.

INNOVATE THROUGH NEIGHBORING

The Great Command—to "love another as I have loved you"—is foundational to the Great Commission. We simply cannot see people embrace the way of Jesus unless they are embraced by our love first. Our US cities are changing fast. Urban culture is now geographically blending into the suburbs and diversifying. Many cities in the US are now becoming more like global cities as urban professionals move downtown and the marginalized move to the edges of the city and suburbs. We have a new opportunity to re-imagine our commuter, "attractional" model of Sunday-drive-in church by listening to the prophetic voice of parish leaders and neighborhood-focused pastors.

We live in a new day. The challenge of creating a bridge between these two worlds geographically, economically, spiritually, and culturally is more crucial than ever. We must learn to be church where we live, work, and play—asking the question, "How can we become family with those we are serving and doing life beside?"

INVITE YOUR CHURCH
TO BECOME "INTENTIONAL NEIGHBORS." [19]

There are many couples or students who long to invest their lives in the great causes of our day. Identify areas in your community where neighbors are needed, or consider connecting your students with Mission Year—a yearlong discipleship program for students ages 18-29.

---

19   For a fuller understanding of "Intentional Neighboring" and "Vocational Neighboring," see the Glossary of Common Terms on page 163.

INVITE BUSINESS PROFESSIONALS
TO BECOME "VOCATIONAL NEIGHBORS."

Churches often create internal "business fellowship networks" that could be flipped outward for the sake of empowering the poor, both locally and globally. What is your church's collective personality? Are we a church of mechanics? Connectors? Entrepreneurs? How could this make-up be used to empower the poor and transform deep pockets of poverty in our neighborhoods?

BE SURE YOUR BUDGET REFLECTS YOUR VISION

A strategic budget can empower intentional action. Consider leveraging your financial resources into community development projects in our urban communities and suburban cul-de-sacs. Invest in the assets that already exist in a given neighborhood, making room for experiments that flow with creative research and expand God's Kingdom.

PURSUE INTERDEPENDENT IMAGINATION

Marco The Poet speaks, "Take the limits off of God because the God you serve is bigger than you can possibly think." [20] We are invited to be part of the new, reconciling family that Jesus came to bring— regardless of social, racial, or economic position. What untapped creativity are we yet to discover in our diversity? The future of healthy neighborhoods is dependent upon our interdependency.

---

20 "Bigger Thank You Can Think" Original Release Date: April 18, 2011, Label: Marco The Poet Productions, Copyright: 2011 Marco Anthony Maltbia, Duration: 2:34 minutes http://www.amazon.com/Bigger-Than-You-Can-Think/dp/B004YBIDO6/ref=sr_1_fkmr0_1?ie=UTF8&qid=1377567209&sr=8-1-fkmr0&key words=marco+the+poet+bigger+than+you+can+possibly+think

GIVE YOURSELF AWAY

While it may sound simple, the reality is that this is quite counter-cultural. Here goes. Build God's Kingdom, not an institution or a brand. Find quiet ways to serve behind-the-scenes, taking the posture of a learner—and a servant. Channel your church's culture of brand toward God's creative love in humility in pursuit of mutual listening, giving and co-investing into relationships that honor the dignity of vulnerable people. Caring about issues of injustice goes beyond a brand. It has always been God's heart.

JUMP IN FOR THE LONG HAUL

Rather than focusing on short-term projects, churches have the most impact when seeking long-term partnerships. The transformation of a neighborhood can take as long as 10-15 years, even beyond our lifetime, and establishing God's shalom requires an ongoing commitment.

BUILD A DIVERSE TEAM

Submitting ourselves to multi-ethnic leadership models is crucial in the Kingdom of God. The future of our changing US landscape is a multi-ethnic world, and Jesus followers everywhere can experience the joy of unity in diversity. Seek to learn from, support, and hire capable, skilled, and strong multi-ethnic teams. Submit to wise, elderly leaders who have gone before us and to the voices of female leaders who round out our limited masculine perspectives. Collectively, we represent the image of God together.

Many churches only focus on providing "relief" and "betterment" service projects and activities—which can be damaging to your church and those you are serving. Seek out the best practices that honor people's dignity. To learn about Christian community development, visit www.ccda.org. You might even want to consider hosting a CCDA Institute at your church.

PRIOR TO STARTING A NEW INITIATIVE

Prior to starting any new initiative, be sure to ask a few core questions:

- Do we sense the Spirit's leading voice here?
- Are we asking the right questions? Do we know our history here?
- Is there an invitation by local leaders, long-term neighbors, or stakeholders?
- Are homegrown neighbors in favor of this project? Is there shared ownership and leadership among neighbors and partners to begin moving forward?
- Are we checking in on a regular basis to be sure we are affirming people's dignity while developing local leaders?
- What are the strengths, gifts, assets, or beautiful characteristics here? How is God already moving here?
- Is there a qualified local visionary (or manager) to get things going? How will local leaders be developed as a result of this new initiative or program?

INDICATORS OF TRANSFORMATIONAL IMPACT

There are many factors that can prohibit the work of transformation that we must be aware of each day. The context of each unique place determines which kind of challenges we will have to confront as we do God's loving work. As we seek transformational impact, some of our challenges might include the following factors:

- The withdrawal of the mainstream church from society
- A need to increase our understanding of spiritual, social, economic, and cultural history
- One's season of life related to time, motivation, personality, or fatigue
- Varying communication styles between people such as written, visual, and oral
- Varying organizational styles between partners such as task-driven, time-oriented, relationally motivated, or other cultural nuances
- Increased isolation and a need for mutual and cohesive partnerships and diverse teams
- The reality of city planning NIMBYism (Not in My Backyward), individual racism, environmental racism, and corporate sin
- Seeing and understanding our need for others
- Broken relationships, distrust of others, or excessive individualism
- Cultural misunderstandings
- Access (or not) to social and economic opportunity

A community's pursuit of transformation takes time. Transformation includes qualitative (relational) and quantitative (numerical) outcomes that work toward inward and outward change, not external performance. Dr. Graham Tomlin reminds us, "Tragically, churches have so often seen these as competing agendas - as if we had to choose between evangelism and social commitment or personal growth. They belong together, and only work when they are together. When it begins to be itself, realizing the grandeur of its calling and the resources available to it from the Spirit, there is nothing on earth to compare with the Church of God."[21]

It is nearly impossible to determine what changes are the direct results of one's involvement, as there are many varied factors that impact the wellbeing of a community. However, neighbors, groups, and churches committed to work together can focus on specific geographic areas, charting changes that occur over time, while channeling activities toward specific outcomes.[22]

While we may never see the results of our involvement, we are called to be faithful. I am reminded of Dr. Martin Luther King, Jr.'s speech, "*Unfulfilled Dreams*,"[23] Where Dr. King calls forth the prophetic voice of Scripture, reminding us that we are told in 1 Kings 8:18, "You did well to have it in your heart." What truly matters is the reality of what exists under the hood, beneath the surface, and behind the veil. Our motives combined with the action of our lives are what matters most. How are we stewarding our lives, resources, and God-given gifts toward love? In the words of Dr. King, "God judges us by the total

21   Tomlin, Graham. The Provocative Church. 3d ed. London: SPCK, 2009, 119.
22   One great resource for improving outcomes is FASTEN. To learn more visit, www.fastennetwork.org or see www.bethelnewlife.org for a core list of measurable categories within a neighborhood.
23   Taken from his audio speech found at http://mlk-kpp01.stanford.edu/index.php/kingpapers/article/unfulfilled_dreams/

bent of our lives." What matters is that we attempt to follow the ways of God, set our hearts right, and walk by faith.

AND FINALLY ...

The effectiveness of our efforts to empower the poor could be significantly enhanced if, prior to launch, would-be helpers would take the following pledge:[24]

I will never do for others what they have (or could have) the capacity to do for themselves.

I will limit my one-way giving to emergency situations and seek always to find ways and means for legitimate exchange.

I will seek ways to empower the poor through hiring, lending and investing and use grants sparingly as incentives that reinforce achievements.

I will put the interests of the poor above my own (or organizational) self-interest even when it may be costly.

I will take time to listen and carefully assess both expressed and unspoken needs so that my actions will ultimately strengthen rather than weaken the hand of those I would serve.

Above all, to the best of my ability, I will do no harm.

---

24   The following pledge is taken from Robert D. Lupton, *Toxic Charity: How Churches and Charities Hurt Those They Help (And How to Reverse It)* (New York: HarperOne, 2011), 128. Used by permission.

We've got some difficult days ahead. But it really doesn't matter with me now. Because I've been to the mountaintop. I don't mind. Like anybody, I would like to live a long life. Longevity has its place. But I'm not concerned about that now. I just want to do God's will.

And he's allowed me to go up to the mountain. And I've looked over, and I've seen the Promised Land. I may not get there with you, but I want you to know tonight that we as a people will get to the Promised Land.

So I'm happy tonight. I'm not worried about anything. I'm not fearing any man.

"Mine eyes have seen the glory of the coming of the Lord."

Dr. Martin Luther King Jr.
"The Measure of a Man"
April 3, 1968

GLOSSARY OF COMMON TERMS

Thriving City Block: A small, defined area known as a supportive, desirable environment; a place marked by caring neighbors who affirm the dignity of all people through love and respect.

Kingdom: Living life under the influence of God's ways—a people marked by justice, mercy, and humility in pursuit of following Jesus as King over all other kingdoms.[25]

Shalom: Peace, wholeness, and joy as right relationship in all of life; God's intention for one's self, others, and creation with anticipation of the future city of God; and the brokenness of all things restored back to wholeness in the peace and presence of God.

Justice: A people in right relationship with God, self, others, and creation both individually and systemically; individuals, communities, institutions, and policies marked by wholeness and righteousness in pursuit of equality, dignity, and the empowerment of all people in all places.

Thriving: Flourishing, sustainable, accessible, connected, safe, and life-giving.

City: Urban geography—blocks, streets, homes, apartments, buildings; inclusive of one's street or place made up of diverse urban people, cultures, and perspectives living within or beyond the city limits.

---

25   I am hesitant to define "Kingdom." While Jesus never gave a clear definition of God's "now/not yet" Kingdom, he described it this way: "The Kingdom of God is like . . . the Kingdom of God is near . . . from another place . . . and from within . . . " (a borderless, boundless, transcendent culture of God's love in motion).

Block: A small focus area surrounded by streets, homes, apartments, and buildings; rooted in geography and connected to one's defined neighborhood, city, and region.

Focus Area: A small four-block radius (or a one mile stretch) where people are committed to mutual friendships, exchanging resources, and living local life together.

Neighborhood: A defined place made up of multiple city blocks where people do life; a social entity, usually defined by geographic boundaries; a place often known by name, culture, history, wealth or struggle; a parish where every home and building, every blade of grass, and every person is meant for a redemptive purpose.

Intentional Neighbors: Faith-motivated people who reside in specific communities to make a significant contribution to the life of a neighborhood; individuals or families who live with intentionality, building long-term relationships among neighbors from all walks of life; neighbors who are known by their resilient love as listeners and learners.

Vocational Neighbors: Businesses or individuals who leverage professional skills, access, and connections for the benefit of under-resourced neighbors, working as a vocational community for the benefit of everyone, including the poor and marginalized.

Under-resourced: A defined focus area that happens to be impoverished, underemployed, disinvested, distressed, disinherited, or economically poor; a struggling neighborhood where approximately 40% of local residents are living below the poverty line or in sub-standard conditions.[26]

Relief Work: Relief is a field of work focused on "stopping the bleeding" during times of extreme emergency, war, trauma, devastation, drought, or the aftermath of severe storms; relief work often requires meeting basic needs such as blankets, food, clothing, water, medical assistance, or emergency funding (often triggered by situational poverty).

Community Development: A field of work focused on increasing the capacity and empowerment of a local people's community, engaging the dreams, hopes, concerns, assets, and strategies of local neighbors by which a community recovers and builds upon its history and future to restore under-resourced neighborhoods or villages (often bound by generational poverty).

Regenerate: A process of people working together over the long haul to transform a neighborhood out of faith, hope, and love; unity, oneness, and beloved community in Christ.

---

26   "Evidence Matters: Understanding Neighborhood Effects of Concentrated Poverty."
U.S. Department of Housing and Urban Development (Winter 2011)
http://www.huduser.org/portal/periodicals/em/winter11/highlight2.html

ADDITIONAL RESOURCES

A FEW COMMUNITIES TO LEARN FROM[27]

Christian Community Development Association (CCDA) offers a CCDA Institute with the following programs: Intensives, Immersion, and Leadership Development Cohorts. CCDA provides a wide range diverse voices and nationally recognized approaches to restoring under-resourced communities and city blocks. And CCDA partners with churches and non-profits to provide on-site training with your community. To learn more, visit www.CCDA.org or write to info@ccda.org.

Communities First Association (CFA) is a professional association of Intermediary Christian Community Developers that provides a supportive learning environment, resources, and tools to those who transform communities. To learn more, visit www.communitiesfirstassociation.org.

Desire Street Ministries (DSM) is an intermediary organization committed to walk beside urban leaders in multiple cities to become thriving and sustainable over the long haul. DSM focuses on leadership health, organizational health, and ministry effectiveness. To learn more, visit www.DesireStreet.org.

---

27   You can find many other communities listed under the "Starting Points" section of the Ten Characteristics of Thriving City Blocks. You can also find a plethora of resources at www.urbanministry.org.

FCS Urban Ministries (FCS) is a collective of urban visionaries and social entrepreneurs in Atlanta, Georgia with a focus on transforming under-resourced neighborhoods. FCS hosts an Open House several times a year. You will hear an array of perspectives, ideas, and strategies, interact with Dr. Bob Lupton and FCS Directors, experience aspects of a local neighborhood, and enjoy selected workshops on community development. To learn more, visit www.FCSministries.org.

InterVarsity's Fresno Institute for Urban Leadership (FIFUL) exists to equip college students to become urban leaders by engaging the Gospel in an inner-city context. Also, be sure to explore Dr. Jim Westgate's Urban Resource Library on the FIFUL website. To learn more, visit www.fiful.org.

Leadership Foundations: The Leadership Foundations network consists of individuals and organizations throughout the world working together to transform their cities through effective leadership. We do this by identifying resources and key players in a city—local grassroots organizations, ministries, and government agencies— that can make the greatest difference to bring about change in the lives of individuals and communities. To learn more, visit www. leadershipfoundations.org.

Mission Year is a yearlong urban ministry program focused on Christian service and discipleship. Mission Year takes teams of people, places them in an area of need, and helps them to serve people and create community. Mission Year is committed to the command of Jesus to "love God and love people," by placing the needs of neighbors first and developing committed disciples of Christ with a heart for the poor. To learn more, visit www.missionyear.org.

New Life Fellowship Church (NLF) is a multi-racial, international church in Elmhurst, New York with over sixty-five countries represented. NLF is a pioneering community for emotionally healthy spirituality, while walking with people toward a commitment to community development among the marginalized of New York City. To learn more, visit www.newlifefellowship.org.

Parish Collective supports neighborhood churches, missional communities, and any group of Christ-followers desiring to be faithfully present in their neighborhood on behalf of parish renewal. People from neighborhoods up and down the West Coast are joining in on behalf of parish renewal. To learn more, visit www.parishcollective.org.

O' LIVING GOD

O' LIVING GOD,

Light and Life

You hold all things together

Beginning and the end

[ALL]

Stir us anew

Awaken us now

Kindle your fire

We love out of your love

We move within your movement

You are behind and ahead

EVER-PRESENT SPIRIT,

You part the sea

Carrying us through

You care for the suffering

Welcoming all

[ALL]

Stir us anew

Awaken us now

Ignite your fire

Healing Hope

Forgiving Friend

Joy and Justice

Holy Presence

Resurrected Christ,

Pursuing each

Gently calling

One family, unified

[ALL]

Stir us anew

Awaken us now

Ignite your fire

Strong invitation

Rock of salvation

Law of liberation

Divine Neighbor,

Good news near

Your Kingdom come

Land and love, together

Beginning, now, forever

[ALL]

Stir us anew

Awaken us now

Ignite your fire

We cry to you

We lift you high

We trust you close

O' Living God,

Amen

An Appeal to Neighbor[28]

Let us lay down our idols
of safety, despair and consumption
as we grab hold of the courage,
hope, and simplicity we long for.

Let us seek justice, mercy, and humility.
As neighbors, we have a choice to make.
We can choose love.
We can choose life—together.

May we imagine creative ways to love
our neighbors where we live and work.
May we find our locations and vocations
bringing life and meaning
to real people in real relationships.

Together,
we must seek out the root causes
that undermine the health of our neighborhoods.

Our opportunity
is to merge our urban and suburban worlds,
socially and professionally,
including the outcast.

Let us rise up and love our neighbor.
We've got some work to do.

---

28   This liturgy was inspired by "An Appeal to March," an invitation calling people
to join the 1963 March on Washington during the Civil Rights Movement.

BIBLIOGRAPHY

Adeyemo, Tokunboh, ed. *The African Bible Commentary: A One-Volume Commentary Written by 70 African Scholars*. 2d ed. Grand Rapids: Zondervan, 2010.

Barber, Leroy. *Everyday Missions: How Ordinary People Can Change the World*. Downers Grove, IL: Intervarsity Press, 2012.

_____. *New Neighbor: An Invitation to Join Beloved Community*. Available online: http://www.newneighbor.org/.

Boone, Dan. *The Church in Exile: Interpreting Where We Are*. Oklahoma City: Dust Jacket Press, 2012.

Bouttier, Michel. *Prayers for My Village: Translated from French by Lamar Williamson*. Nashville: Upper Room, 2005.

Brueggemann, Walter. *Using God's Resources Wisely: Isaiah and Urban Possibility*. Louisville: Westminster John Knox, 1993.

_____. *The Prophetic Imagination*. 2d ed. Minneapolis: Fortress Press, 2001.

Canada, Geoffrey. *Fist, Stick, Knife, Gun: A Personal History of Violence*. Rev ed. Boston: Beacon Press, 2010.

Carroll R., M. Daniel. *Christians at the Border: Immigration, the Church, and the Bible*. Grand Rapids: Baker Academic, 2008.

Chandler, Paul-Gordon. *God's Global Mosaic: What We Can Learn from Christians Around the World*. Downers Grove, IL: Intervarsity Press, 2000.

Chester, Tim, ed. *Justice, Mercy, and Humility: Integral Mission and the Poor*. Milton Keynes, UK: Paternoster, 2003.

Dyson, Michael Eric. *Know What I Mean?: Reflections on Hip-Hop*. New York: Basic Civitas Books, 2010.

Elmer, Duane. *Cross-Cultural Conflict: Building Relationships for Effective Ministry*. Downers Grove, IL: InterVarsity Press, 2005.

ESV Urban Devotional Bible. Wheaton: Crossway Books, 2007.

Freire, Paulo. *The Pedagogy of the Oppressed*. 30th Anniversary Edition. New York: Bloomsbury Academic, 2000.

Fisman, Raymond, Rakesh Khurana, and Edward Martenson. "Mission-Driven Governance." *Stanford Social Innovation Review Vol. 7, No. 3* (Summer 2009).

Fountain, John W. True Vine: *A Young Black Man's Journey of Faith, Hope, and Clarity.* Cambridge: PublicAffairs, 2005.

_____. *Dear Dad: Reflections on Fatherhood.* Chicago: WestSide Press, 2011.

Galvin, James C. "Strategic Plans That Learn: An Innovative Alternative to Traditional Strategic Planning." *Outcomes Magazine* (Summer 2010): 20-2.

Gilliam, Alex. "Building Blocks: What LEGOs can teach us about rebuilding cities." No pages. Cited 26 February 2012. Online: http://grist.org/cities/building-blocks-what-legos-teach-us-about-rebuilding-cities/.

Gordon, Wayne L. *Who is My Neighbor?: Lessons Learned From a Man Left for Dead.* Ventura: Regal Books, 2010.

Green, Gary, Anna Haines, and Stephen Halebsky. *Building Our Future: A Guide to Community Visioning.* Madison, WI: Cooperative Extension Publications, 2000.

Hale, Matt, and Beverly Hale. "A Bible Study in Righteousness and Justice." Good Works, Inc. Online: http://www.good-works.net/PDF_Files/A_study_in_Justice_and_Righteousness.pdf

Hanleybrown, Fay, John Kania, and Mark Kramer. "Channeling Change: Making Collective Impact Work." No pages. Cited 26 January 2012. Online: http://www.ssireview.org/blog/entry/channeling_change_making_collective_impact_work.

Haugen, Gary A. *Just Courage: God's Great Expedition for the Restless Christian.* Downers Grove, IL: InterVarsity Press, 2008.

Hoang, Bethany H. *Deepening the Soul for Justice.* Downers Grove, IL: InterVarsity Press, 2012.

Hunsberger, George R. and Craig Van Gelder, eds. *The Church Between Gospel and Culture: The Emerging Mission in North America*. Grand Rapids: Eerdmans, 1997.

Ishac, Allan. *New York's 50 Best Places to Find Peace and Quiet*. 6th ed. New York: Universe, 2011.

Jacobs, Jane. *The Death and Life of Great American Cities*. 50th Anniversary Edition. New York: Modern Library, 2011.

Jacobsen, Eric O. *Sidewalks in the Kingdom: New Urbanism and the Christian Faith*. Grand Rapids: Brazos, 2003.

_____. *The Space Between: A Christian Engagement With The Built Environment*. Grand Rapids: Baker Academic, 2012.

Jenkins, Philip. *The Next Christendom: The Coming of Global Christianity*. 3d ed. New York: Oxford University Press, 2011.

Jones, Sally-Lloyd. *The Jesus Storybook Bible*. Grand Rapids: Zondervan, 2007.

King Jr., Martin Luther. *The Measure of a Man*. Minneapolis: Fortress Press, 2001.

Kling, Fritz. *The Meeting of the Waters: 7 Global Currents That Will Propel the Future Church*. Colorado Springs: David C. Cook, 2010.

Kretzmann, John P., and John L. McKnight. *Building Communities From the Inside Out: A Path Toward Finding And Mobilizing A Community's Assets*. Chicago: ACTA Publishing, 1993.

Labberton, Mark. *The Dangerous Act of Loving Your Neighbor: Seeing Others Through the Eyes of Jesus*. Downers Grove, IL: Intervarsity Press, 2010.

Linkner, Josh. *Disciplined Dreaming: A Proven System to Drive Breakthrough Creativity*. San Francisco: Jossey-Bass, 2011.

Livermore, David A. *Cultural Intelligence: Improving Your CQ To Engage Our Multicultural World*. Grand Rapids: Baker Academic, 2009.

Lowney, Chris. *Heroic Leadership: Best Practices from a 450-Year-Old Company That Changed the World*. Chicago: Loyola Press, 2005.

Lupton, Robert D. *Theirs Is The Kingdom: Celebrating the Gospel in Urban America*. New York: HarperOne, 2011.

_____. *Toxic Charity: How Churches and Charities Hurt Those They Help (And How to Reverse It)*. New York: HarperOne, 2011.

Lynch, Fred D. *The Script: A Hip Hop Devotional through the Book of John*. Grand Rapids: Zondervan, 2008.

Lyons, Gabe. *The Next Christians: Seven Ways You Can Live the Gospel and Restore the World*. Colorado Springs: Multnomah, 2012.

Marsh, Charles. *The Beloved Community: How Faith Shapes Social Justice from the Civil Rights Movement to Today*. New York: Basic Books, 2005.

Martin, Jim. *The Just Church: Becoming a Risk-Taking, Justice-Seeking, Disciple-Making Congregation*. Carol Stream: Tyndale Momentum, 2012.

Metzger, Michael. *Sequencing: Deciphering Your Company's DNA*. Waukesha: Game Changer Books, 2010.

Muller, Wayne. *Sabbath: Finding Rest, Renewal, and Delight in Our Busy Lives*. New York: Bantam, 1999.

Myers, Joseph R. *The Search to Belong: Re-thinking Intimacy, Community, and Small Groups*. Grand Rapids: Zondervan, 2003.

Nelson, Mary. *Empowerment: A Key Component of Christian Community Development*. Bloomington, IN: iUniverse, 2010.

Nouwen, Henry J. M. *In the Name of Jesus: Reflections on Christian Leadership*. New York: Crossroad, 2010.

Palmer, Parker J. *A Hidden Wholeness: The Journey Toward an Undivided Life*. San Francisco: Jossey-Bass, 2009.

Park, Sydney M., Soong-Chan Rah, and Al Tizon, eds. *Honoring the Generations: Learning with Asian North American Congregations*. Valley Forge: Judson Press, 2012.

Perkins, John, ed. *Restoring At-Risk Communities: Doing it Together and Doing It Right*. Grand Rapids: Baker Books, 1996.

Rah, Soong-Chan. *The Next Evangelicalism: Freeing the Church from Western Cultural Captivity.* Downers Grove, IL: InterVarsity Press, 2009.

Rickett, Daniel. *Making Your Partnership Work: A Guide for Ministry Leaders.* Enumclaw, WA: WinePress Publishing, 2002.

Scazzero, Pete. *Daily Office: Remembering God's Presence Throughout the Day.* Chicago: Willow Creek Association, 2009.

Schlabach, Joetta Handrich. *Extending the Table: Recipes and stories of people from Argentina to Zambia in the spirit of More-with-Less.* Scottsdale, PA: Herald Press, 1991.

Sherman, Amy L. *Kingdom Calling: Vocational Stewardship For the Common Good.* Downers Grove, IL: InterVarsity Press, 2011.

Shinabarger, Jeff. *More or Less: Choosing a Lifestyle of Excessive Generosity.* Colorado Springs: David C. Cook, 2013.

Smith, Efrem. *Raising Up Young Heroes: Developing a Revolutionary Youth Ministry.* Downers Grove, IL: InterVarsity Press, 2004.

Smith, Efrem and Phil Jackson. *The Hip Hop Church: Connecting with the Movement Shaping Our Culture.* Downers Grove, IL: InterVarsity Press, 2006.

Smith, Gordon T. *Courage and Calling: Embracing Your God-Given Potential.* Rev ed. Downers Grove, IL: InterVarsity Press, 2011.

Spencer, Aida Besancon and William David Spencer, eds. *The Global God: Multicultural Evangelical Views of God.* Grand Rapids: Baker Academic, 1998.

Stern, David H. *The Jewish New Testament Commentary: A Companion Volume to the Jewish New Testament.* Clarksville, MD: Jewish New Testament Publications, 1992.

Thurman, Howard. *Jesus and the Disinherited.* Boston: Beacon Press, 1996.

Tomlin, Graham. *The Provocative Church.* 3d ed. London: SPCK, 2009.

Tutu, Desmond. *An African Prayer Book*. New York: Doubleday, 2006.

_____. *Children of God Storybook Bible*. Grand Rapids: Zondervan, 2010.

Vanier, Jean. *From Brokenness to Community*. Mahwah: Paulist Press, 1992.

Wheeler, Houston. *Organizing in the Other Atlanta: How the McDaniel-Glenn Leadership Organized to Embarrass and Lead Atlanta's Pharaohs to Produce Affordable Housing in the Community*. Southern Ministry Network, 1992.

Wilson Jr., Paul. *Dream B.I.G. in 3D: How to Pursue a Bold, Innovative, God-Inspired Life!* Kennesaw: ParaMind, 2009.

Wright, Tom. *The Meal Jesus Gave Us: Understanding Holy Communion*. Louisville: Westminster John Knox, 2002.

Yedinak, George. "Top Ten Trends in Senior Housing for 2013." No pages. Cited 7 January 2013. Online: http://seniorhousingnews.com/2013/01/07/top-10-trends-in-senior-housing-for-2013/.

ACKNOWLEDGEMENTS

And in honor of my wife, Melissa Ledbetter, whose love and life inspires me with joy, this project is dedicated to my children, who I pray will grow up to love their neighbors well:
Selah, Shiloh, Levi, and Zeke.

Today, I remember all those who are risking their lives, reputations, and relationships for the sake of God's Kingdom of faith, hope, and love. I remember those who are being imprisoned and violently oppressed, those being baptized behind closed curtains, and those who may never get to experience life on a thriving city block. Together, let us not grow weary in doing good.

This resource is a reflection of principals and lessons I am learning over the course of my vocational journey. Many neighbors and friends continue to speak into my life through their patient mentoring, and I thank God for the beauty of God's diverse community. This work is an extension of countless leaders known and unknown, those off the beaten path, and those carrying the name of Jesus in hard places.

And this project is only made possible through the collective wisdom of FCS Urban Ministries, as well as many other voices throughout CCDA (Christian Community Development Association). I am deeply grateful to all the members of the South Atlanta community, especially to our neighbors on Thirkield Ave, in Atlanta, Georgia.

I also owe much gratitude to family, friends, and mentors along the way: Fred and Marsha Sweet (aka, "Mamma Sweet"), Darryl Ledbetter, John and Andrea Nelson, Brian and Linda Mayfield, Rev. Stacey Foster, Brad and Becky Cannon, Eric Campbell, Tracy and Jenna Commons, Paul McGuinness, Anthony and Dionne Cox, Brian

Hyma, Dr. Ed Dobson, Rev. Marvin Williams, the late Rev. Dante Alighieri Venegas, Dr. Tandy Champion, Rev. Earl James, Dick and Betsy DeVos, Ed and D. Marie Strain, Keith and Suzanne Sparzak, Dr. David Stoner, Steve MacLurg, Rob Bell, Matt Krick, Kathy Christensen, Denise VanEck, Sean and Sarah Alsobrooks, Mark and Carolyn Baas, Dan and Adrienne Crain, Andrew and Annette Richards, Dwight Gibson, Samuel Chiang, Dale and Karen Cross, Danny and Jessica Wuerffel, Dr. Anthony Gordon (aka, "The Quiet Riot!"), Sara Pace, Angie Winn, Ebonie Sanders, Elizabeth Richards, Rev. David Park, Dr. Daniel Rickett, the Osterink family, James and Alison Slone, Ed Sohn, Jason and Kristi Garcia, Dr. Amy Sherman, David Kim, Mo Thomasos, Todd Harrison, Doug Vander Meulen, Dr. Rob Hughes, Paul Wilson, Jr., Rev. Leonce Crump II, Mr. Totem, Dr. Steve Hayner, Jeff Shinabarger, Rev. Chris Etheridge, Bryson Volgeltanz, Derek Sweatman, Miss Rachel Barber, Dr. Betty Palmer, Rudy Carrasco, Shane Claiborne, Miss Mary Porter, Jared Faellaci, Ken Steel, Richard Stamper, Cohort #2!, Rev. Brian Wangler, Chicago First Church of the Nazarene, Coach Wayne Gordon, Noel Castellanos, Dr. Bethany Harris, Rev. Jonathan Brooks, and our neighbors in the Austin neighborhood of Chicago, Illinois.

And a deep thanks to:

My editor, Mike DeVries, for your friendship and brilliant insights.

Caleb Seeling: For believing in the vision early on.

Joe Fioramonti: For your creativity marked by prayer.

John Topliff: For the generosity of your wisdom.

Diane Hitzfeld: For reading and re-reading with grace and foresight.

Wendy Butts: For your praying, fasting, and believing.

Andrej Ciho & Billy Quezada: For the talks.

Tracy Commons: For speaking truth and standing with me.

Dan Crain: Your encouragement and humor keep me sane.

Bob and Peggy Lupton: This project is a result
of your patience and guidance.

Leroy and Donna Barber: I continue to learn so much from you.

Danny Wuerffel: You stood by my side when the going got tough.

John Booy: Your example marked me for life. I have few words.

Jeff and Ruth Bell Olsson: Thank you for your friendship.
What a journey, eh?

Mamma Sweet: For leading me to Jesus at your bedside
at the age of six.

Melissa,
I thank God for the gift of this walk together.
You are truly amazing.

ABOUT NATE

Nate Ledbetter is an explorer, bridge-builder, storyteller, and urban minister at heart. He is greatly impacted by the people he has met throughout his global travels and urban living, and he is passionate to apply the love of neighbor in every context, including urban development, vocational neighboring, and practical theology. He and his wife, Melissa, and their four children reside in the Austin neighborhood of West Side Chicago, where Nate serves as pastor of Church on the Block, linked with Chicago First Church of the Nazarene. He enjoys writing, basketball, beatbox, and sharing in life's crazy stories.

Nate served as a Local Outreach and Regional Pastor for six years at Mars Hill Bible Church in West Michigan before relocating to Atlanta, Georgia, to join FCS Urban Ministries, an urban collective made up of multiple organizations dedicated to restoring under-resourced communities. While in Atlanta, he served as co-executive director of FCS and created Metro Merge, a non-profit division of FCS. He also served with Desire Street Ministries to encourage urban leaders toward becoming thriving and sustainable.

Nate is a member of the national board of directors of the Christian Community Development Association (CCDA) and is a certified trainer of CCDA. He holds an MA from Grand Rapids Theological Seminary and is a CQ-certified facilitator via the Cultural Intelligence Center. He could eat guacamole and chips everyday of his life, and is available to speak to a group in your context.

LET'S CONNECT

To suggest an idea, share a story from your city block,
or to connect with Nate: **www.ThrivingCityBlocks.com**

---

nate@thrivingcityblocks.com
www.AwakenNeighbor.com
Twitter @awaken_neighbor
Facebook.com/nateledbetter

Picture taken by Andrew D. Hoffman of www.myneighborlink.org

www.THRIVINGCITYBLOCKS.com